The Diaper Bag Book for Babies

W9-BPK-959

Authors

Robin Dodson and Jan Mades, M.A.

Editor-in-Chief: *Sharon Coan, M.S. Ed.*

Editorial Project Manager: *Mara Ellen Guckian*

Publishers: *Rachelle Cracchiolo, M.S. Ed.*
Mary Dupuy Smith, M.S. Ed.

Product Manager: *Phil Garcia*

Illustrators: *Blanca Apodaca, Kevin Barnes, Janice Kubo*
Kelly McMahon, Renée Christine Yates

Art Manager: *Kevin Barnes*

Art Directors: *Lee Aucoin, CJae Froshay*

Imaging: *James Edward Grace, Rosa C. See*

Cover Design: *Neri Garcia*

Teacher Created Materials, Inc.
6421 Industry Way
Westminster, CA 92683
www.teachercreated.com

©2004 Teacher Created Materials, Inc.
Made in U.S.A.
ISBN #0-7439-3757-0

Table of Contents

Introduction

You are your child's first and most important teacher. The roots of social, emotional, physical, and cognitive development lay in the security and acceptance your baby experiences in his relationship with you. It is in the context of this supportive relationship that your baby can take the risks necessary to learn. As your baby grows from infancy to toddlerhood, you set the tone for your child's feelings of confidence and competence as he faces challenges. A baby who has been provided with a variety of activities, allowed to experience success, encouraged to try again, and loved regardless of his performance, will develop the attitude and skills that promote growth in all areas of development.

Most of the activities in this book require little or no materials and can be done at the spur of the moment. Keeping up with an ever-changing child does not leave much time for elaborate plans. It is in the unfolding of your everyday life that your baby does most of his learning.

Babies learn best through repetition and imitation. The suggestions in this book will provide many opportunities for exploration, discovery, and trial and error. With you nearby, your baby will feel secure enough to try new things, make mistakes, and celebrate his accomplishments. Your baby will respond to your encouragement and acknowledgement of his efforts with increasing confidence. You will be developing the foundational skills to meet his potential at any age.

How to Use This Book

This book is arranged by developmental stages. The specific month when each child passes a developmental milestone is not as important as the sequence of skills that determine the level at which the child functions. Occasionally a baby may skip a particular skill, but most babies follow the same sequence.

The activities are grouped in loose categories of active or quiet play. During a typical day, active play opportunities present themselves when a baby is well rested and well fed. Feel free to try activities from the preceeding developmental stage. Babies need to practice things again and again before they can feel a sense of mastery. Babies need to do a task and do it well before a new accomplishment occurs. Repetition is a way of life.

If your baby can already do an activity well, adjust it to provide a little more challenge. Many of the activities list variations to adjust the difficulty. Keep in mind that babies have short attention spans so they may not finish one thing before going on to something else. Expect variation in interest level and ability to focus. Keep playtime fun. Relax and follow your baby's lead. She will develop skills sometimes because of what you do, and sometimes despite what you do.

The greatest gift you can give your baby is the support she needs to become the person she was meant to be, according to the inner timetable she is following. Have fun and know that the simple everyday activities you share will provide a strong foundation for the years to come.

Cuddlers
Newborn to Five Months

The newborn is a little overwhelmed adjusting to life. Baby's schedule can be erratic and unpredictable. As you and your infant become more familiar with each other, a rhythm of alertness and rest develops. Soon, you will recognize the subtle signals of an infant in an alert state, ready to eat or interact, versus an infant who is over-stimulated and needs to shut down and rest. The alert state will increase to include periods of playing and smiling. Patterns of daily life are emerging.

A cuddler's body movements seem unintentional and full of sudden jerks. As you learn which body positions your infant prefers, help him calm himself by helping him assume those positions. Some babies love to suck and accept a pacifier. Visual babies like to be held upright. They take in the sights as you walk through the house. Many babies need rhythmic motion like gentle bouncing, swaying, or swinging. All these methods help your baby transition to a calm state and develop self-soothing behaviors as he gets older.

Cuddlers have fully developed hearing and close-range vision at birth. The cuddler learns to recognize the voices of his parents and loves looking at faces from 8 to 12 inches away. Developing trust is the number one task of the infant. Responding quickly and consistently to his cries establishes that your baby can elicit and rely on help from you to get his needs met.

Creepers
Four to Nine Months

During the creeper stage, little ones are working on developing regular patterns of sleeping and eating. The day will soon come when your infant doubles his weight and can sleep for a period of five to eight hours. You emerge from the fog of sleeplessness and can now begin to shape more regular patterns of sleep and alert cycles. With the introduction of solid foods, a regular "mealtime" is added to the daily routine. This also creates opportunities for more enriched play, language development, and self-awareness.

The creeper is able to keep her head off the ground and soon will be able to roll over from any direction. She gains control of gross movements of her arms and legs. By the end of this stage, a creeper can purposefully kick at a toy to make it move or can move her arms to bat at, and later grab, the toy.

Babies can now imitate facial expressions and begin to make gurgling and cooing sounds. These pre-verbal skills are the beginning of language. A parent is now convinced that it is not just gas but a real smile that your baby is giving you as you gaze into each other's eyes.

Crawlers
Six to Eleven Months

Babies in the crawler stage will master a sense of balance that will allow them to sit without help. The baby will be able to roll across the floor in purposeful movements and may be able to push himself from the floor into a sitting position. Many babies love to stand up for long periods of time. Some visual babies prefer to be in a vertical position. This is a very good time to encourage crawling movements. Some babies like to drag their bodies across the floor in commando fashion. Others will begin to rise up on all fours and rock back and forth. Soon they will be crawling across the room.

Crawlers are also gaining skills in the area of fine motor development. They are beginning to practice picking things up, with their fingers and thumb in a modified palmer grasp, holding them as if they were wearing mittens.

Babies at the crawler stage are able to babble with distinct consonant plus vowel patterns. Sometimes you can even hear a distinguishable word like "bye" or "dada." The infant may not connect these first words with the objects yet, but they are practicing the sounds. Babies talk with their eyes at this age. If you say a word that a baby knows, he will follow (track) with his eyes to the object you named. Or, he will look and maybe even point to something he wants. This is real communication. It is absolutely essential that parents follow up on pre-verbal attempts at talking.

Cruisers
Ten to Fifteen Months

Cruisers can crawl rapidly, but they really love to pull themselves up into a standing position. They can use most anything above them to pull to a stand and will walk around furniture or use a push toy to begin taking steps. They prefer holding onto fingers at first, but before they leave this stage they will be able to walk independently. Cruisers are "into everything." You will need to rethink your baby-proofing strategies. Cruisers need many opportunities to explore. You will be more successful at keeping your baby safe by altering the environment (remove floor lamps that can tip over, put away breakable knickknacks) than expecting baby to understand "no" and stop herself.

Cruisers' fine motor skills are changing as well. Babies will move from a palmer grip to a more defined pincer grasp that uses the thumb and first and second finger to pick up very small objects.

Sometime during this period your baby hits a major milestone: a REAL word. He will use that word to manipulate his environment. "Doggie" can refer to any four-legged creature. "Juice" can get a drink of water or milk. But this is true use of language communication when baby can make commands and have her needs met.

Climbers

Twelve to Eighteen Months

Climbers are very confident in their improving motor skills. They walk, run, and climb in, on, and over everything. They explore their surroundings with deep curiosity and zeal. Objects are mouthed, banged, carried, dropped, and fitted inside each other. A climber can pull books from a shelf, empty a cupboard, and take apart a room. You need to provide for lots of safe exploration; it is what climbers want.

Climbers develop a broad receptive vocabulary and can follow simple directions. Most of their expressive vocabulary is still single words. Their inability to communicate their more complex thoughts can easily frustrate climbers.

Climbers show growing independence in feeding skills. They like to "help" you with dressing and other simple routines. Climbers feel most confident when their day follows familiar routines and you are within sight. Your baby can be playing independently, but if you leave the room he will cry and follow you. He still needs a lot of emotional support as he starts to grapple with being a separate person.

Areas of Development

Reinforcing Daily Routines

Routines and rituals that are repeated over time are the foundation for important brain development. Order in our external world promotes order in our minds. (For example, some people can't relax until the house is straightened up.) It is by living through known routines that a baby learns how to recognize patterns and anticipate what happens next. This is her first experience with sequencing, an important reading and math skill. Having a familiar schedule throughout the day also helps her gain a sense of control over her life. She does not need to be in a constant state of concern by not knowing what will happen next. Routines build security. Repetition builds mastery.

Social-Emotional Development

Everyday, care-giving situations make way for social and emotional growth. Establishing a bond between parent and child is essential for later positive mental health. Developing a secure attachment between parent and child allows the infant to learn that the world is safe. This will eventually result in high self-esteem, the ability to separate from parents, and independence. But first, an infant must learn that her parents will respond to her needs. This primary relationship establishes trust for the rest of the child's life. A baby who can communicate a need that gets met learns that she is valued and worthy of others' loving care. When the baby's physical and emotional needs are met consistently, she can turn her attention to exploring her world. Deep independence grows from deep dependence.

Areas of Development (cont.)

Gross Motor Development

Gross motor development refers to any activity that requires the coordination of movements of the body's large muscles. The development of gross movements precedes the development of smaller, refined movements. Infants gain control of movement from the head downward to their feet, and from the center of the body outward. In this sequence, babies typically gain head control, then torso control to turn their bodies over. First, they wildly swing their limbs, and then they refine it to an intentional kick or grasp of an object. The sequence continues from rolling over to sitting up to crawling, and finally walking.

Fine Motor Development

Fine motor development refers to any movement that requires the coordination of the muscles in the wrists, hands, fingers, and sometimes shoulders. These skills are required to pick up tiny objects, stack small blocks, feed one's self, manipulate toys, and eventually having enough control to grasp a crayon or pencil properly. There is a specific sequence of movements that the baby must master. First is a *palmer grasp* that uses the entire fist to close over an item, similar to using mittens. Next, the hand can use an index and second finger to grasp objects to the thumb. This grasp becomes more defined until a *pincer grasp* is fully developed, using only the thumb and pointer finger. Fine motor skills are also necessary to learn to talk. The tongue and facial muscles allow for pronunciation of the sounds required for clear speech.

Areas of Development (cont.)

Sensory Development

Sensory stimulation is raw input for the brain. Sights, sounds, tastes, textures, and smells bombard baby constantly. Baby will learn to differentiate between unfamiliar and known sensations. New sensory experiences give her more information to process and categorize. A baby must have the sensory experience before she will associate and understand the words that go with it. She will not understand the words *cold*, *rough*, or *red* until she has had many experiences with those sensations.

Cognitive Development

Cognitive development refers to the development of thinking skills. Early cognitive skills include the following concepts:

- object permanence
- spatial awareness skills that encompass visual tracking and visual discrimination
- building memory
- making associations
- recognizing *same* and *different*
- early symbolic thought (knowing a picture represents a real object)

Areas of Development (cont.)

Language Development

Communication starts at birth with cries and eye contact. Babies learn gestures and attribute meaning to sounds. (The door closing means Daddy is home. The microwave beep means lunch is ready.) They learn to attend to the spoken word above the background noise in their environment. Pre-verbal skills require a baby to isolate the sounds of a word from the stream of language going on around her. The baby must then associate the right sound sequence to the right object. Looking at a named object is a language skill, so is pointing to an object. Receptive language, the ability to understand words spoken to you, is developed before expressive language, the ability to say words.

Typically, baby's first word appears around 12 months. Almost every activity in this book involves introducing your baby to the language of her home country. Some parents may have the advantage of speaking two different languages. If each parent speaks to the child in his or her given language, the child will grow up to be proficient in both languages. Expressive milestones may be reached a little later. For example, the first words may be said closer to the second birthday than the first birthday, but your child will learn pronunciation and grammar before she is five without ever having to take a language class!

Baby Dumpling

Baby's skin is delicate and can dry out easily. Apply a good quality unscented body lotion to protect it. Use the following nursery rhyme to make a game out of this routine.

Baby, Dumpling

Baby, baby dumpling, boiling in a pot
(Warm lotion by rubbing it in your hands first.)

Sugar him and butter him
(Apply lotion liberally.)

And eat him while he's hot.
(Kiss that cute baby!)

Materials: baby lotion

Developing Skills

- tactile stimulation
- face-to-face bonding

Jeremiah, Blow the Fire

This is a "naked baby" rhyme perfect while changing a diaper or during dressing.

Jeremiah, Blow the Fire

Jeremiah, blow the fire—puff, puff, puff
(Blow three little puffs on your baby's tummy.)

First you blow it gently
(Blow a long, sustained, gentle blow.)

Then you blow it rough!
(Blow a big gust.)

Developing Skills

- tactile stimulation
- face-to-face bonding

Materials: none

Little Rattlesnake

Little Rattlesnake

As I was walking near the lake,

(Walk your fingers up your baby's leg or arm.)

I met a little rattlesnake.

(Draw continuous "S" curves on the baby's tummy.)

He ate so much of jelly cake,

(Tap baby's cheeks.)

It made his little belly ache.

(Pat or tickle baby's tummy.)

Developing Skills

- tactile stimulation
- face-to-face bonding

This is another "naked baby" rhyme perfect while changing a diaper or during dressing.

Materials: none

Tickle Me

Playing "Tickle Me" is one of the joys of parenting. Give your cuddler different experiences with touch by creating a "tickle glove." Take an odd glove and attach different fabrics to each finger. Place the glove on your own hand and let the baby grasp at each of your fingers in turn. Softly stroke your baby's bare arm or leg with one texture at a time. Stroke her tummy or cheek. Talk about the feel of different textures (e.g., fur, silk, corduroy, cotton balls). **Variation:** Use a new feather duster or fuzzy rubber ball on your baby's skin.

Developing Skills

- sensory exploration
- tactile stimulation
- language development

Materials: an old cloth glove, fabric scraps that vary in texture, glue

Self Talk

The first year of a baby's life is a huge investment period in his language development. You will talk almost constantly to him; he won't say a recognizable word back for almost a year, and then he'll pronounce it incorrectly! Self-talk is narrating your activity while baby watches so he can connect the words to what he sees. "I'm putting on my coat. One arm in this sleeve, one arm in that sleeve. Here's a shoe. It goes on my foot. Now, I will tie my shoe. There, all done." This may feel silly at first, but this is a powerful language stimulation tool.

Materials: none

Developing Skills

- language stimulation
- face-to-face bonding

Brow Binky

Brow Binky

Brow binky,
(Gently stroke baby's forehead with the tip of your index finger.)

Eye winky.
(Continue stroking along under each eye.)

Chin choppy,
(Tap baby's chin twice.)

Cheek cherry.
(Stroke each cheek.)

Mouth merry,
(Trace baby's lips.)

Kiss!
(Kiss your baby, of course!)

Materials: none

Infants thrive on skin-to-skin contact. This rhyme focuses on the face. It is perfect for quiet alert time when you can hold your baby close and gaze into each other's eyes. Go slowly and speak softly.

Developing Skills

- tactile stimulation
- auditory stimulation
- face-to-face bonding

Visual Stimulation

Developing Skills

- visual stimulation
- visual tracking

From birth, infants can focus on objects about a foot away. Bright patterns with high contrast hold his attention the best. Use these designs to help your infant develop visual tracking skills. The best way to do this is with minimal words, so your infant can pay attention to the visual information without distraction from your voice.

Hold the design on this page about a foot (30 cm) away from baby's face. Slowly move it to the right. Do baby's eyes follow it? Slowly move it to the left. Return it to the center, and let baby stare at it. Watch for cues that he is losing interest or is overstimulated. If baby is willing, show him another pattern from the following page.

Materials: patterns (pages 21–22)

Visual Stimulation (cont.)

Visual Stimulation Board

Make your baby something to look at, so he isn't quite so squirmy while on the changing table. Even if you can't draw, you can do this. Draw concentric circles, stars, spirals, happy faces, checkerboard patterns, etc. on sturdy white cardboard or poster board. Use a black marker to make thick and thin lines in your designs. Glue on snippets of aluminum foil. Make a second board for the car. Pin it to the upholstery so baby has something to look at while in the rear-facing car seat.

Variations: Use pictures of faces from magazines; add color to your designs.

Materials: white poster board, black marker, foil, glue, magazines

Developing Skill

- visual stimulation

Follow That Sound

Sit behind your baby, out of view, as he lies on his back. Lean down to one side and whisper his name. Does baby turn to look for you? Now try the other side. "Come find me over here, baby." Smile when he finds you and encourage him to do it again. Repeat as long as your baby is interested.

Variation: Use a rattle or squeaky toy to vary the sound. Do not talk to baby, so he can concentrate on one sound at a time.

Materials: a toy that makes noise

Developing Skill

- auditory tracking

Crinkle Sock

This toy makes an unusual sound, unlike store bought toys. Draw a face or make a colorful caterpillar pattern out of the sock. Wash out the snack chip bags and stuff them loosely in the sock. Tie a knot in the end of the sock. While baby is young, you can squeeze the sock for him. Soon he will reach for the sock, hold it, and make the noise himself.

Materials: clean, adult-size tube sock, colorful permanent markers, 3–4 snack-size chip bags

Developing Skills

- auditory stimulation
- grasp and release

Sock Scents

Stimulate your baby's sense of smell with these ideas. Dab a cotton ball with any of the following: vanilla or peppermint flavor extracts, a floral perfume, or essential oils like lavender or eucalyptus. Place the cotton ball in a clean, light-colored sock. Draw a face or design on the sock if you wish. Tie the the end of the sock closed. Hold the sock near your baby's nose. Use rich descriptive language (e.g., "This smells sweet," or "Cinnamon is spicy.") After the scents fade away, wash the sock, and replace the cotton ball with a different scent.

Variations: Remember to expose your baby to scents in the kitchen. Hold up freshly sliced citrus fruits, spice bottles, etc. for your baby to smell.

Materials: various perfumes or scented oils, a clean sock, a permanent marker

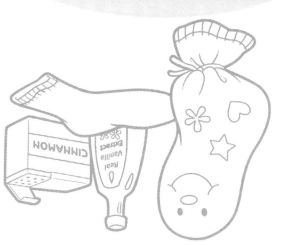

Developing Skills

- sensory stimulation
- vocabulary enrichment

Look Up Here

Give your cuddler time on his tummy every day. She may not tolerate it for very long. Try just a few minutes several times a day rather than one prolonged session. Encourage your baby to stay in this position longer by holding a favorite toy first in front of him and then above his head. A toy with bright visual interest and an unusual sound works best. Offer verbal support. "Look up here. That's it, lift your head. You are getting so strong. Look what you can do."

Materials: favorite toy

Developing Skills

- neck strength
- visual tracking
- auditory tracking

Copycat Game

Minutes after birth your baby is ready for conversation. He will give you subtle signals when he is ready to communicate. His eyes will become shiny and will follow you wherever you move. His hands open and move as though to reach out to you. Sometimes his eyebrows will raise and he may even smile.

Now it is time to play the copycat game. See if your baby will mimic your expressions. Try sticking out your tongue or raising your eyebrows and see if your baby will copy you. Show him a surprised look and see if his face looks surprised, too. It is truly amazing; without looking into a mirror, your baby will become a mirror of your face.

Materials: none

Developing Skills

- self-awareness
- visual memory
- social-emotional development
- expressive language

Water Bottle Toy

Wash out a plastic bottle and remove the label. Fill it about three-quarters full with water. Add a few drops of food coloring to tint the water. Add some glitter or colorful, shiny confetti items. Secure the cap on the bottle by adding some glue to the lid before you twist it back on the bottle. Let the glue dry.

You now have a wonderful shaker toy that will change as the baby makes it move. At first, you will manipulate the toy for your baby. Later, as your baby becomes more capable, he will be able to grasp it, knock it over, roll it, or kick it.

Variations: Use corn syrup or vegetable oil instead of water. Use coins, beads, snippets of sponge, paper clips, etc., to vary the experience.

Materials: clear plastic 1-liter beverage bottle (12 to 20 oz.), food coloring, glitter, tiny shells, etc., waterproof glue

Developing Skills

- spatial awareness
- sensory exploration
- visual tracking
- eye-hand coordination

Reading With Infants

It is never too early to make reading a part of your day. Infants benefit from the warm contact with you. They hear your voice and follow the pictures with their eyes. Cradle baby in your lap, his back against your chest. Now both of you can see the pictures. Most board books for infants have one picture per page. Say that word repeatedly in different sentences. "Apple. Here is an apple. That apple is red. We eat apples. Someday you'll try applesauce." The repetition helps your baby make the association. You get bonus points for holding up a real apple next to the illustration. If you are nursing your baby, reading to your baby is a great bonding activity for Dad to share.

Materials: board books

Developing Skills

- visual tracking
- voice recognition
- pre-literacy skills
- bonding

Cooing and Babbling

Baby's first vocalizations are called cooing. Babies utter vowel sounds like "oooooooooo" and "aaaaaaah." Stimulate language acquisition by simply cooing back! Hold your baby about one foot from your face and repeat baby's sounds back to him. Your soft, lilting voice, eye contact, and eager smile will encourage your baby to reply. Be a good listener. Wait for his answer before cooing back again. Baby learns that his voice is a powerful tool in relationship building. When baby adds consonant sounds, babbling starts. Continue with the call and response game.

Variation: You can initiate the game by cooing or babbling first.

Materials: none

Developing Skills

- language stimulation
- face-to-face bonding
- social development

Playback

Record your cuddler's cooing. Play it back for him. It will encourage him to talk more. Continue to tape the sounds he makes as he grows. He will enjoy hearing them and you will have a precious keepsake to treasure years from now. He won't believe it was him making those funny sounds when you play it when he's three or four years old!

Materials: tape recorder

Developing Skills

- language stimulation
- self-awareness
- social development

Self Esteem Builders

(Sing this song to the tune of "Twinkle, Twinkle Little Star.")

I love you just the way you are

I will help you meet your needs

Feed you, hold you, keep you warm

Offer comfort all day long.

You belong here in my arms

I will keep you safe from harm.

Developing Skills

- self esteem
- face-to-face bonding
- trust

Babies form ideas about themselves based on the way that they are treated. Self esteem is a belief that you are worthy of love and that you belong. This is conveyed in the sensitive, responsive care that baby receives from you and your attitudes about giving that care. Your baby needs to feel "My needs are important," "I am lovable just as I am," and "I belong here." Affirm this in your baby by giving him the care he needs willingly, even at three in the morning. Try this little song, or make up a special one of your own.

Materials: none

Active Play

Nursery Rhymes, Poems, and Songs for Active Play

Each of the following activities provides language, motor, cognitive, self-concept, and bonding experiences. As your baby listens to the words, he is exposed to rhyme, rhythm, and repetition. These "three Rs" are rich language-building tools. In the context of a lap game, your baby will learn a word such as "up" by hearing it and experiencing it. This multi-sensory approach helps reinforce the concept. He will exercise his small and large muscles while trying to coordinate his movements. He learns about himself as you reference his body parts. Through the repetition he also starts to remember, make associations, and anticipate what comes next. These are early cognitive skills. Best of all, time spent in quality face-to-face interactions help build the loving bond that will be the foundation for future interpersonal skills.

Adapt the movements in the rhymes, poems, and songs to fit your baby's development. Early activities for your cuddler have him on a blanket on the floor in front of you. Place him on his back. As he gains head control and likes to be upright, add the sitting games. Adapt how much neck and torso support baby needs by adjusting how you hold him. Avoid vigorous bouncing and tossing baby in the air, as these can cause neck and brain injury similar to Shaken Baby Syndrome.

Little Bear

Little Bear

'Round about there sat a little bear.

(Draw circles with your index finger on baby's tummy.)

One step, two steps

(Walk fingers up baby's chest toward armpit.)

Tickle under there!

(Tickle under baby's arm.)

Developing Skills

- tactile stimulation
- vocabulary enrichment
- face-to-face bonding

Position baby on his back when saying this rhyme. Repeat the verse, using the baby's other underarm. **Variations:** Walk your fingers under baby's chin or behind his knees. When your child is sitting up, you can draw the circle in his palm and walk up his arm to his chin.

Materials: none

Bumblebee

Bumblebee

Bumblebee, bumblebee

(Slowly circle the bee to and fro. Watch baby's eyes follow it.)

Buzzing in the air

(Make a buzzing sound.)

Coming to get your nose right there!

(Move in slowly, and touch baby's nose with the bee.)

Make a simple bee stick puppet. Cut an oval about three inches long (7.5 cm) and two inches wide (5 cm) from bright yellow paper. Use a black marker to draw a face at one end and broad vertical stripes along the rest of the bee's body. This creates a high contrast pattern that is easy for your baby to see. Tape it to a craft stick. Hold the bee about ten inches (25.4 cm) from baby's face. As he gets older and his vision improves, move the bee farther away. Use this rhyme to play a visual tracking game.

Variations: Substitute nose with head, ear, tummy, arm, etc.

Materials: yellow paper, black marker, tape, craft stick

Hickory Dickory Dock

Developing Skills

- tactile stimulation
- face-to-face bonding

Give your baby whole-body tactile stimulation while sharing this rhyme.

Hickory Dickory Dock

Hickory, dickory, dock,
(Alternately squeeze baby's feet in tempo, right, left, right.)

The mouse ran up the clock!
(Walk fingers up baby's left leg to chin.)

The clock struck one,
(Circle baby's face with index finger, tap head once.)

The mouse ran down,
(Walk fingers down right leg.)

Hickory dickory dock
(Alternately squeeze baby's feet in tempo, left, right, left.)

Additional verses: Continue with "the clock struck two," tapping baby's head twice.

Materials: none

Hot Cross Buns

This rhyme creates an opportunity for cross lateral movement of the arms. It takes special coordination to cross your right arm to the left side of your body and vice versa.

Lay baby on his back. Let baby grip your index fingers, one in each hand.

Hot Cross Buns

Hot cross buns, hot cross buns!
(Cross your baby's left arm over his right, then his right over his left, repeat.)

One a penny, two a penny, hot cross buns!
(Continue criss-crossing arms as you lift them over your baby's head.)

Materials: none

Cross Across

Developing Skills

- gross motor coordination
- cross lateral movement
- face-to-face bonding

Lay your baby on his back. Hold his hands or let him grasp your fingers.

Cross Across

Cross to the left

(Bring both of baby's arms to the left side of his body.)

Cross to the right

(Cross both arms over to the right side of his body.)

Lift your arms out of sight

(Raise baby's arms above his head.)

Cross them up

(Cross right arm over left.)

Cross them down

(Cross left over right as you bring the arms back down to the front.)

You're the cutest baby in town!

Knees Go Up and Down

Knees Go Up and Down

Knees Go Up and Down

Your knees go up and down,
Your knees go up and down,
High ho the derry oh,
Your knees go up and down.

2nd verse: **Your feet go in and out...**
(Hold the baby's feet and move them apart and together.)

3rd verse: **Your hips roll side to side...**
(Hold baby's hips and tip him to the right and to the left.)

Developing Skills

- large muscle movements
- body part identification
- face-to-face bonding

Position your baby on his back and sing the words to the tune of "The Farmer in the Dell." Hold the baby's ankles and push his knees toward his chest on the word "up." Extend the baby's legs back down again on the word "down." **Variations:** Add the second and third verses as your baby demonstrates comfort with the song.

Materials: none

Stretch Your Legs

Give your baby a whole-body workout with this song sung to the tune of *"Mary Had a Little Lamb."* Start with baby on his back.

Developing Skills

- gross motor coordination
- range of motion and flexibility
- vocabulary enrichment
- face-to-face bonding

Stretch your legs now up and down, up and down, up and down.

(Hold baby's thighs and alternately lift and lower his legs at the hip joint.)

Stretch your legs now up and down, This is how we move.

(Continue as above.)

Additional verses:

Tip your hips now side to side.

(Roll baby's hips back and forth.)

Bend your knees now round and round.

(Use a bicycle motion when moving baby's legs.)

Raise your arms now high and low.

(Lift baby's arms overhead and back down.)

Spread your arms now out and in.

(Open baby's arms wide, and return to center.)

Sit Ups

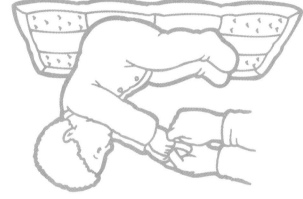

Use your cuddler's natural tendency to tightly grasp objects in his fists to help him strengthen his neck and torso. Lay him on his back facing you. Let him grasp your thumbs while you hold around his wrists and slowly pull him up to a sitting position. With practice he will be able to lift that big heavy head! After a few months he may like pulling to a stand. Always encourage him with your words and facial expressions.

Materials: none

Developing Skills

- neck and torso control
- face-to-face bonding

Dickery, Dickery, Dare

Dickery, Dickery, Dare

Dickery, dickery, dare

(Bounce baby gently on your lap, holding his torso under his arms.)

The pig flew up in the air.

(Lift the baby above you.)

The man in brown soon brought him down.

(Return the baby to your lap.)

Dickery, dickery, dare.

(Bounce the baby gently.)

Developing Skills

- large muscle control of torso
- vocabulary enrichment
- face-to-face bonding

Seat baby on your lap, gently supporting his head and neck.

Materials: none

To Market to Market

To Market, To Market

To market, to market, to buy a fat pig
(Bounce baby with a gentle rhythm.)

Home again, home again, Jiggety-jig.
(Bounce baby with a short, quick pattern.)

To market, to market, to buy a fat hog
(Bounce baby with a gentle rhythm.)

Home again, home again, Joggety-jog.
(Bounce baby with a slow, bumpy pattern.)

Developing Skills

- large muscle control of torso
- exposure to tempo

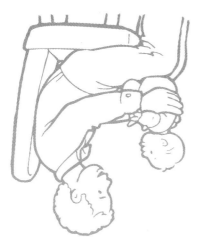

Sit the baby in your lap. Support your baby's torso under his arms or see if baby can support himself while you hold his hands.

Materials: none

Peek-A-Boo

Parents in every culture all over the world play peek-a-boo. It is such an important activity because it helps babies understand 'object permanence': the concept that an object which is no longer visible still exists. You will find variations of this game throughout this book. The first way to play this game is to use a transparent material, such as netting, a sheer scarf, or veiling-type cloth. This way your baby will feel the sensation of the material on his face but he can see through it and know his parent has not disappeared.

Drape the scarf over your baby's face and say the words *peek-a-boo* when you pull the scarf off the baby's face. Play this as many times as the baby seems to enjoy it.

Materials: sheer scarf

Developing Skills

- object permanence
- self-awareness
- sensory stimulation

Wiggly Hair Puppet

Draw a face with black marker on the palm of a glove. Add color to the finger sections. The face will pop out when you open your fist and wiggle your fingers (hair). If you name your puppet you can say, "Here comes Sammy. He's going to get you." Then tickle your baby with the puppet.

Variations: Play visual tracking games. Play "peek-a-boo" type activities.

Materials: a light colored cotton glove (Try inexpensive garden gloves or work gloves sold at hardware stores.)

Developing Skills

- visual stimulation
- visual tracking
- tactile stimulation
- object permanence

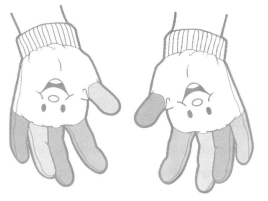

Foot Pushers

Lay baby on his back. Place your hands against the bottom of baby's feet and exert light pressure so his knees bend. Do this when baby is alert and playful and he will push against your hands to straighten his legs. Repeat the motions as long as your baby enjoys them. Offer verbal encouragement: "Push, push, baby. Your legs are getting stronger. That's the way. Look what you can do! Let's do it again."

Variation: Do this when baby is on his tummy to prepare him for scooting and crawling.

Materials: none

Developing Skills

- gross motor coordination
- body awareness
- bonding

Keeping a Naptime Log

Babies sleep a great deal of the day. Develop a specific place to take naps. It will help shape the infant's ability to form a rhythmic pattern of awake and sleep times. Pay attention to how your baby gets his body to relax. Does he like you to rock him and hold him tight? Does he prefer to be left alone and stretch out his body? Perhaps he likes to rock in the swing?

His eyes can help you distinguish if he is ready to settle or if he needs more play time. Take your clues from your baby. Offer naptime when you see those droopy eyes. Write on your daily calendar which method worked for that day. What time did he go down? How long did he sleep? Is there a pattern?

Materials: daily calendar or journal

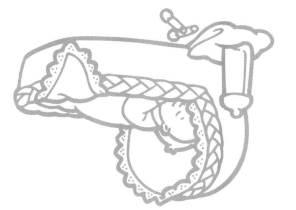

Developing Skills

- social development
- reinforcing routines

Sleep, Baby, Sleep

This gentle nursery rhyme is perfect for bedtime. Substitute your baby's name to personalize it.

Sleep, Baby, Sleep

Sleep, baby, sleep.
Thy father guards the sheep.
Thy mother shakes the dreamland tree,
And from it falls sweet dreams for thee.
Sleep, baby, sleep.

Sleep baby, sleep,
Down where the woodbines creep.
Be always like the lamb so mild.
A kind and sweet and gentle child,
Sleep, baby, sleep.

Developing Skills

- self-calming routines
- face-to-face bonding

Naps and Bedtime

Cuddlers

Helping Baby Settle

Every baby is unique. Each will develop his own way to calm down. Watch for cues and then help the baby use his way. At first, this will be just trial and error. Parents must be willing to watch and wait. Give baby opportunities to develop and practice a preferred method. A little time spent fussing allows baby to work at discovering success on his own. Sometimes a combination of methods works best. Baby's preferences will get more recognizable as he gets older.

The three typical ways a baby settles are either sucking, vision, or body motion/position. Sucking is a rhythmic behavior. A baby will try to suck on his wrist, the back of the hand, or his fist. Eventually, some babies rotate their hands so they can suck on fingers or thumbs. A visual baby will settle by shutting out visual stimuli, focusing on a wall or a white wall or a window with a distant view. A baby who prefers motion will need to move his arms in a windmill pattern as he becomes stressed. By concentrating on watching his hands he can block everything else out and settle down. Other babies prefer not to get caught up in movement. They settle when you keep them swaddled firmly so their arms and legs cannot escape. Only observation will help a parent decide which method, or combination of methods, will help settle the cuddler to sleep.

Helping Baby Settle (cont.)

Settling a Baby that Prefers to Suck

A baby who likes to suck to settle himself is easy to recognize. This little cuddler usually falls back asleep as soon as he receives the bottle or breast. He is not really hungry, he is after comfort. He will usually take a pacifier. Help the baby find a wrist, fist, or finger to begin to suck on. This may be all the encouragement he needs to begin to find a way to settle himself down. Baby can't lose his fingers in the middle of the night the way he can lose a pacifer.

- Position baby so he can get to his hand.
- Do not cover his hands with sleeves or mittens.
- File, clip, or cut baby's nails to keep his face protected.

Developing Skills
- self-awareness
- eye-hand coordination
- social-emotional development
- trust

Helping Baby Settle (cont.)

Settling a Visual Baby

As early as 3–4 weeks a baby may begin to select what he likes to focus on and what he prefers to avoid. A visual baby may become overwhelmed with the intensity of a face-to-face interaction and choose to turn away to keep from being stressed.

- Late in the day, carry baby facing away from your body.
- To help him settle himself down during the night, have a night-light on.

Developing Skills

- self-awareness
- social-emotional development
- trust

- Choose visual targets that involve distant vision or diffused light.
- Do not talk at the same time you are looking at the baby.
- Keep your face off to one side rather than fully centered.
- Minimize noise and handling that may distract baby. But remember, picking him up may help him open his eyes to choose a focus spot.

Helping Baby Settle (cont.)

Settling a Baby Who Prefers Motion or Body Position

Motion or lack of it may help your baby settle down. Some babies like being swaddled in a blanket to keep their motion to a minimum. Others prefer to have their arms left free to move about. Behavioral cues about body position and motion preferences are the most difficult to determine.

- Do not move baby from an awkward-looking body position if baby is content.
- Do not assume that all babies prefer to be contained in a swaddling position.
- If baby prefers to move his arms, do not hold him tightly; it will make him more agitated.
- Try stroking with a gentle constant pressure on baby's back as opposed to patting.
- Temporarily place the baby on his tummy so he can settle himself. Never leave him in this position to sleep. After he has calmed down, swaddle him in a blanket and lay him on his back for sleeping.

Developing Skills

- self-awareness
- social-emotional development
- trust

Coping With Crying

Sometimes babies cry for no identifiable reason. If you are sure he isn't wet, hungry, too cold or hot, or lonely, know that it isn't your fault. When a baby is overtired or over-stimulated you may have limited success in calming him down.

If nothing seems to work, take a break before your frustration and anger build. You can put baby in his crib for 10 minutes. Use this time to calm yourself. Get a drink of water, put a cool cloth on your forehead, massage the back of your neck, call a friend, or close your eyes and take some deep breaths. If baby is still crying, pick him up and try to soothe him again for 20 minutes. Take another break if you need it. If this happens frequently, check with your doctor to rule out medical causes.

Materials: none

Developing Skills

- reinforcing routines
- trust

Infant Massage

Communicate with your baby in a way she understands: use the language of touch. Massage is a wonderful way to connect and express love to a baby. Following her cues of readiness make this a pleasurable experience for both of you. Adjust your pace, the time you spend, the number and type of strokes you choose, and the pressure of your touch according to the messages your baby sends you. There is no one right way to do massage. It is a shared experience that needs to feel right for both of you. Try these basic strokes after bath time, an hour or so before her "fussy" time, or first thing in the morning. Prepare a warm spot with low lighting. Add gentle music if you wish. Use good quality body oil or lotion specifically designed for massaging baby skin. Take a few deep breaths yourself, take the phone off the hook, and focus on your baby. No one can communicate your loving touch the way you do. In general, start with the major areas of the body. The chest or back is a good place to start. Massage the legs before working on the feet or toes. Do full strokes on the arms before attending to the hands and fingers. You don't have to do all the strokes or all parts of the body in one session. Experiment with what your baby likes.

Massage Strokes

Milking

Lay baby on her back facing you. Cup your hand around the outside of your baby's leg, near the buttocks. Stroke down her leg toward her feet. Alternate this milking movement with your other hand on the inside of her leg. Continue over hand for several strokes. Repeat with the other leg.

Variation: These same strokes can be used on the arms, starting at the shoulder and working toward the wrist.

Developing Skills

- tactile stimulation
- bonding

Squeeze and Twist

Cup both your hands around your baby's leg near her buttocks. Alternately squeeze and twist your hands while slowly moving from her hip toward her ankle. Repeat with the other leg.

Materials: lotion or oil (optional)

Massage Strokes (cont.)

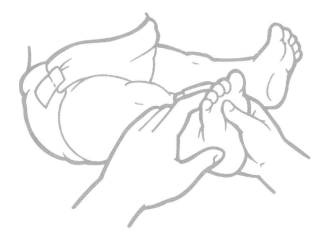

Thumb Over Thumb

Stroke the sole of your baby's foot down the center from heel to toe with your thumbs, one after the other in a continuous cycle. Repeat with the other foot. You can also stroke the top of the foot this way, moving toward the toes.

Squeeze and Wiggle

Support your baby's foot in one hand, and gently squeeze and rotate each toe separately.

Variation: Do "Thumb Over Thumb" on the palm or back of your baby's hand. Try "Squeeze and Wiggle" on her fingers.

Materials: lotion or oil (optional)

Developing Skills

- tactile stimulation
- bonding

Massage Strokes (cont.)

Water Wheel

Paddle the pinky side of your hands down baby's stomach in a hand over hand continuous motion. Start below the ribs and progress to the lower abdomen. Apply gentle pressure. This may aid in baby's digestion and help her release gas.

Thumbs Apart

Place the full length of your thumbs on baby's stomach near her belly button. Gently press and stroke outward toward her sides.

Materials: lotion or oil (optional)

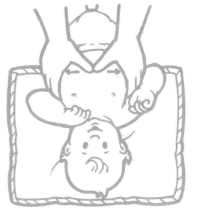

Developing Skills

- tactile stimulation
- bonding

Massage Strokes (cont.)

Open Heart

Using the flats of your hands, make a heart shape on your baby's chest by starting in the center of the breastbone, moving outward and downward, ending above her belly button.

Cross your Heart

Start with both hands at the base of your baby's rib cage. Slide your right hand up and across her chest to baby's right shoulder and then slide it back down to the starting position. Slide your left hand up to your baby's left shoulder and back down. Repeat several times, alternating hands.

Materials: lotion or oil (optional)

Developing Skills

- tactile stimulation
- bonding

Massage Strokes (cont.)

Combing

Use your fingertips to stroke down your baby's back, starting at the neck and ending at her buttocks. Gradually lighten your touch as you repeat this stroke, ending with the lightest touch.

Back and Forth

Sit to the side of baby. Start with both hands at the top of your baby's back. Slide your hands across the baby's back, side-to-side, alternately in opposite directions. Progress down the back to the buttocks.

Materials: lotion or oil (optional)

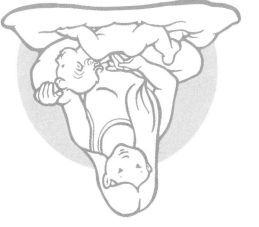

Developing Skills

- tactile stimulation
- bonding

Crying as Communication

The creeper's favorite activity is seeking social interaction. Babies prefer faces to any other object given them. Soon you will discover that your creeper uses her cry for other messages besides eating. Don't assume that every time you hear your creeper cry that she wants to eat. Develop a checklist to respond to your baby in different ways before you offer the bottle.

If the attempts suggested in the column to the right have no settling effect, then of course, offer her nourishment.

Developing Skills

- pre-verbal communication
- bonding
- self-awareness

- Try talking to her. She may just want to hear your voice.

- Try rubbing her back. She may want to feel your touch.

- Try looking into her face and talking. She may be in the mood for a real conversation.

- Try rolling her into a position where she can get to her hand in case she wants to suck.

- See if she needs a dry diaper.

- Pick her up and walk to the window so that she can see the world.

Materials: none

Changing Table Song

Try singing these words to the tune of "Twinkle, Twinkle, Little Star."

Changing Table Song

Change a diaper just like this,

When you have a little mess.

First pull off your little pants,

Then the diaper, and the mess.

Wash and put dry diaper on.

Pants back on, it's time for fun.

Developing Skills

- reinforcing routines
- body awareness
- language development

Baby is becoming more aware of her surroundings. It is good to establish routines. Always bring baby to the changing table for diaper changes. It will be easier for her to understand what is happening. It is important to describe to her what you are doing. If you have a song to sing she will be able to anticipate what to do next and be able to determine when you will finish.

Materials: none

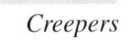

Changing Table Mobile

Creepers become more interested in complex, multicolored visual items. It may be time to remove the mobile from the crib so baby will have less stimulation at night when she is fatigued. Don't put it away; just move the mobile to over the changing table. This can become part of your routine as you change your baby. Sing the changing song (page 62) as you bring her over for a change. Get everything ready before laying her down. Since your creeper can turn over, this can be a dangerous situation. Be prepared. Turn the mobile on and finish the change. Baby will be more focused and less squirmy.

Materials: mobile

Developing Skills

- auditory stimulation
- visual tracking

Teething Remedies

Some creepers are beginning to develop teeth. For some this is an easy process. For others, teething can be a time for discomfort. Here are a few ideas to ease the process. Store a wet cloth in a resealable bag in the freezer. Remove the chilled cloth from the bag and give it to your creeper to chew on. Be sure to place a bib on her. As she chews on the cloth, it will melt and leave her wet.

Materials: face cloth, resealable bag

Developing Skills

- tactile stimulation
- social development

Solid Foods

Developing Skills

- eye-hand coordination
- grasp and release
- tactile stimulation

Introduce your baby to the social joys of eating supper as a family. Swallowing food is different than swallowing formula or breast milk. Expect to have more on the outside than the inside when you first begin. Keep a hand on the bowl or buy one that has a suction cup on the bottom. Start with baby cereal. As you introduce vegetables and fruits, do so one food at a time. When you are ready to try meats, know that you will probably have to mix it with one of her favorites, maybe applesauce or carrots. Creepers are very sensitive to texture. It may take several attempts before she will accept a different food. Don't give up, just keep offering at each meal. Everything takes practice.

Materials: solid foods, bowls, spoons, bibs, baby wipes

Baby's Own Spoon

When you start solid foods, let your baby hold her own spoon. She isn't quite ready to feed herself, but she can practice holding it. She can learn to associate the spoon with eating. The day will come when she will try to put it in her mouth (probably upside down). At some point, she will not want you to feed her, insisting on doing it herself. Keep mealtime relaxed by letting baby explore the textures of her food with both her mouth and her hands. These are all healthy steps toward independence.

Materials: baby spoon, solid foods, bowl, bib

Developing Skills

- eye-hand coordination
- self-help skills
- sensory motor exploration

High Chair Time

When your baby is sitting up comfortably, the high chair can become a play station too. Baby will enjoy watching you work at the sink from this vantage point. If you are washing dishes, let baby hold a spoon or plastic cup. Put a little water on the high chair tray for her to pat and splash. If you are washing vegetables, put a potato or carrot on the tray for her to examine. Name the objects for her and narrate your activities. When you are done, ask your baby if she wants to get down. Look for some indication, a reaching gesture or a sound, that you can reinforce as communication.

Materials: kitchen items

Developing Skills

- language stimulation
- social interaction
- visual tracking

Reach for the Sky

When offering your baby a toy to hold, make sure you vary its position. Hold it way over to the left or to the right. Hold it above her head. This encourages baby to reach, and to use eye-hand coordination. Try this: if baby reaches with her left hand when the toy is offered on her left side, move the toy across to her right side. Does she still reach with her left hand or does she switch to her right hand? Cross-lateral movement requires a lot of coordination.

Materials: toy

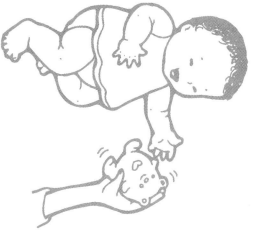

Developing Skills

- eye-hand coordination
- torso balance
- cross-lateral movement

Not Enough Hands

When baby is sitting up, hand her a small toy. Offer her a second toy. Now, get her attention and hand her a third toy. What does baby do to solve this problem? Some babies drop one item to get the third, some babies try to hold two things in one hand, and some babies reach for the third item with their mouths. There is no right answer. What would your baby do with a fourth?

Materials: 3 toys

Developing Skills

- problem solving
- eye-hand coordination
- grasp and release

Not Just Mozart

Brain research shows that classical music stimulates the area of the brain used for mathematical thinking. But music is so much more than that. Expose your baby to lots of different styles of music. Share music from different genres, different cultures, and different artists. Listen to your favorites and dance with baby. Hold her and spin, sway, and step to the beat.

Materials: different musical selections

Developing Skills

- bonding
- rhythm and tempo
- exposure to music

Here Are Your Ears

This body poem gives baby an all over tactile experience while naming several body parts.

Here Are Your Ears

Here are your ears. Here is your nose.
(Touch baby's ears, then her nose.)

Here are your legs. Here are you toes.
(Shake baby's legs and touch her toes.)

Here is your chin. Here are your lips.
(Tap your index finger on her chin, then her lips.)

Here are your knees, Here are your hips.
(Shake her knees back and forth and roll her hips side to side.)

Developing Skills

- body awareness
- tactile stimulation
- face-to-face bonding

Variation: Substitute other body parts. The parts do not need to rhyme.

Materials: none

Who's That Baby?

Materials: safety mirror

Developing Skills

- self awareness
- face-to-face bonding

Your baby will enjoy playing in front of a mirror. She doesn't know that she is seeing herself. Since it is nice to have a playmate that enjoys the same things you do, lay a full-length mirror on its side against a wall. Put something in front of it at the ends to prevent it from tipping over. Place baby and some toys on a blanket in front of the mirror. Get down on the floor and make faces too. Name the people in the mirror.

Out the Window

Hold your baby up to a window and talk about what you see when you look outside. This works particularly well if you have a regular "event" to see each day. Maybe it's birds at the feeder in the morning, the letter carrier delivering the mail, the school bus picking up kids at the corner, or Daddy or Mommy pulling out of the driveway to go to work. Describe what you see to help baby focus on the scene.

Materials: none

Developing Skills

- vocabulary enrichment
- visual stimulation

Grand Old Duke of York

The grand old Duke of York,
he had ten thousand men.
(Bounce baby on your knees.)

He marched them to the top of the hill,
(Lift baby by drawing your knees up.)

And he marched them down again.
(Lower baby by dropping your knees back down.)

And when you're up, you're up.
(Lift up again.)

And when you're down, you're down.
(Lower again.)

And when you're in the middle,
you are neither up nor down.
(Raise your knees half way and sway them side to side, then lower them.)

Creepers are ready for more vigorous motions. Follow baby's cues: Does she like the bouncing? going faster? going slower? Sit on the floor with your legs outstretched. Try this rhyme, holding baby in a sitting position on your knees, facing you.

Developing Skills

- torso control
- abdominal work for Mom or Dad!
- balance
- vocabulary enrichment

This is the Way

Here is a great lap-bouncing game. Sit baby facing you. Hold her hands, or for more support, hold her under her arms.

Variations: Alternate the words so the ladies ride fast and the gentlemen ride slowly. Change the words "ladies" and "gentlemen" and "farmers" to "mommies" and "daddies" and "babies" or other appropriate words.

Materials: none

Developing Skills

- torso control
- balance
- vocabulary enrichment
- exposure to tempo

This is the Way the Ladies Ride

This is the way the ladies ride:
Trit, trot, trit, trot.
(Bounce in small quick rhythm.)

This is the way the gentlemen ride:
Jiggety jog, jiggety jog.
(Bounce more vigorously.)

This is the way the farmers ride:
Hobblety hoy, hobblety hoy.
(Alternately lift and lower each knee to tip baby side to side.)

This is the way the hunters ride:
Gallopy, gallopy, gallopy,
(Quicken the pace.)

Over the fence!
(Lift baby high above.)

See Saw

Sit your baby facing you on the floor positioned between your legs. Hold her hands as you rock back and forth. On the word faster, speed up, and repeat the poem.

See Saw, Margery Daw

See saw, Margery Daw,
Jackie shall have a new master.
He shall have but a penny a day,
Because he can't work any faster.

Materials: none

Developing Skills

- torso control
- balance
- vocabulary enrichment
- exposure to tempo

Row Your Boat

Row Your Boat

Row, row, row, your boat

(Hold baby's hands. Slowly pull baby up to a sitting position.)

Gently down the stream.

Merrily, merrily, merrily, merrily,

(Pull baby forward and push back while rocking back and forth.)

Life is but a dream.

Developing Skills

- abdominal strength
- neck strength
- vocabulary enrichment

This is a wonderful activity to do when your baby has more energy than you do. Either lay the baby on the ground or sit the baby down with support behind her back. The baby should be facing you. Hold her arms to help her with the movements. **Variation:** Some babies will want to be pulled to a standing position.

Materials: none

Rock Your Boat

Here's an alternate version to "Row, Row, Row, your Boat." Sit baby in your lap facing you.

Rock Your Boat

Rock, rock, rock your boat.
(Tip baby side to side throughout the song.)

Rock it to and fro.

Rock, rock, rock your boat.

Over the side you go!
(Tip baby way over.)

Materials: none

Developing Skills

- torso control
- balance
- vocabulary enrichment

Humpty Dumpty

Humpty Dumpty

Humpty Dumpty sat on the wall.
(Gently sway back and forth.)

Humpty Dumpty had a great fall.
(Lower yourself to the ground and roll back on your back.)

All the king's horses,
And all the king's men

Couldn't put Humpty together again.
(Roll back to a sitting position.)

Developing Skills

- balance
- vocabulary enrichment
- gross motor coordination

Give your baby a full-size ride with this rhyme. Do this on a carpeted surface. Start in a standing position with baby in your arms against your chest.

Materials: none

Flying Man

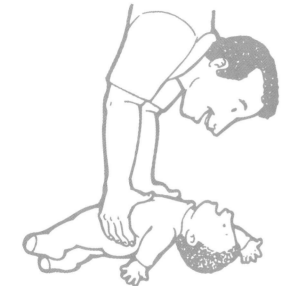

Flying Man

Flying man, flying man, up in the sky
(Lift baby up by extending your arms above you.)

Where are you going to, flying so high?
(Tip baby to the right and to the left.)

Over the mountains, and over the sea
(Lift your baby up and down.)

Flying man, flying man,
Won't you take me?
(Lower your baby back down.)

Developing Skills

- torso control
- balance
- vocabulary enrichment

Trot, Trot

Sit toward the edge of a chair or couch. Sit your baby in your lap facing you.

Trot, Trot to Boston

Trot, trot to Boston, trot, trot to Lynn.

(Bounce baby up and down.)

Look out baby, you might fall in!

(While holding baby, spread your legs and lower her through them.)

Trot, trot to London, trot, trot to Dover

(Bounce baby up and down.)

Look out baby, you might fall over!

(Tip baby over the side of your lap.)

Materials: none

Developing Skills

- torso control
- balance
- vocabulary enrichment

Mix a Pancake

Position baby in your lap for this rhyme.

Mix a Pancake

Mix a pancake.
(Jiggle baby lightly.)

Stir a pancake.
(Roll baby's hands around each other.)

Pop it in the pan.
(Clap baby's hands together.)

Fry a pancake.
(Drum {sizzle} your fingers on baby's tummy or head.)

Toss a pancake.
(Lift baby up.)

Catch it if you can!
(Lower baby back to your lap.)

Developing Skills

- torso control
- balance
- vocabulary enrichment

Peek-A-Boo

You have been playing this game with a transparent cloth. Now you can use a more solid type of fabric. This time the scarf goes over mommy or daddy's face. The parent says "peek-a-boo" and removes the scarf. Enjoy the look of surprise on your baby's face when she sees you are under that scarf. Sing the little chant: Where is mommy? Here I am!

Materials: scarf

Developing Skills

- object permanence
- self-awareness
- vocabulary enrichment

Jingle Socks

Ride a Cockhorse to Banbury Cross

Ride a cockhorse to Banbury Cross
To see a fine lady upon a white horse.
(Gently bounce baby in your lap.)

With rings on her fingers
(Touch baby's fingers.)

And bells on her toes,
(Shake baby's foot.)

She shall have music wherever she goes.
(Continue bouncing.)

Developing Skills

- auditory tracking
- awareness of feet

Sew a jingle bell on each end of a pair of baby's socks. Baby will discover the sounds she makes when shaking her feet and will soon do this on purpose. Say the rhyme as baby shakes her feet. **Caution:** Always supervise baby when she is wearing her jingle socks. She may put them in her mouth. If the bells came loose, they would pose a choking hazard.

Materials: Clean pair of baby's socks, 2 large jingle bells, a needle and thread.

Bell Horses

Bell horses, bell horses,
What time of day?
(Bounce baby in your lap.)

One o'clock, two o'clock,
(Shake one foot then shake both feet.)

Up and away!
(Lift baby up.)

Developing Skills

- torso control
- balance
- auditory stimulation

This English nursery rhyme refers to a mechanical clock with horses that chime the hours. It is perfect for jingle socks.

Materials: none needed, bells or jingle socks are an option

Jingle at the Door

This rhyme works equally well with baby laying on her back or sitting in your lap.

Jingle at the Door

One, two, three, four,
Jingle at the front door.
(Shake baby's right foot.)

Five, six, seven, eight,
Jingle at the back gate.
(Shake baby's left foot.)

Developing Skills

- gross motor coordination
- exposure to counting
- auditory stimulation

Materials: none needed, bells or jingle socks are an option

Kick, Kick, Kick

Lay your baby on her back. Tuck a rolled towel under her tailbone to support her and help keep her legs up. Put a handful of dried beans or rice inside a balloon before you blow it up. Suspend the inflated balloon on a string above her feet. Encourage her to kick it. She may kick more with vigorous marching music playing to stimulate her.

Caution: Balloons that are not inflated and popped balloon pieces are serious choking hazards. Always supervise this activity and put the filled balloon away when not in use.

Materials: balloon, dried beans or rice, string, rolled towel

Developing Skills

- eye-foot coordination
- gross motor play
- auditory stimulation

Hop Little Bunny

Hold your baby up under her arms and suspend her just above the floor. Bounce her gently so her feet "hop" against the floor. Tell her to "Hop like a bunny. You're doing it! Hop, hop, hop! There you go, little bunny." Soon she will intentionally push against the floor.

Materials: none

Developing Skills

- gross motor coordination
- leg strength

Tummy Time

Roll a bath towel into a thick cylinder. Prop your creeper on it, with the roll across her chest, up under her arms. Place a variety of toys in front of her within her reach. With her hands free to explore, she will tolerate tummy time a little longer. This position also gives her a fresh perspective of her surroundings.

Materials: bath towel, toys

Developing Skills

- neck strength
- torso strength
- reaching with hands

Cardboard Can Time

Make a toy from a potato chip can to encourage baby to hold her head up while on her tummy. Wash out the can and the plastic lid, and then cover the can with decorative shelf paper.

Next, start saving the metal lids from frozen juice cans. Lids need to have rounded edges. (Juice can lids pop off when you release the plastic around the edge of the can. They have no sharp edges.) The lids are large. They are not a choking hazard and can be mouthed safely. The metal lids fit inside the small cardboard can and will make a lot of noise when shaken. Baby can bat at the can and knock it over to hear the sound.

Materials: potato chip can (regular size or individual serving size), juice can lids, shelf paper

Developing Skills

- auditory stimulation
- eye-hand or eye-foot coordination
- cause and effect
- visual tracking

Five in the Bed

Help your creeper get the sensation of rolling over with this traditional song. Position your baby on a small blanket laying on a soft surface like the middle of your bed or a thick carpet.

Materials: small blanket

Developing Skills

- gross motor coordination
- anticipation
- spatial awareness

Five in the Bed

There were five in the bed and the little one said,

"Roll over, roll over"!

So they all rolled over and one fell out.

(Lift one side of the blanket up to gently roll baby over.)

There were four in the bed and the little one said,

"Roll over, roll over"!

So they all rolled over and one fell out.

(Lift the other side of the blanket up to roll baby the other way.)

Continue with additional verses: three in the bed, two in the bed, and so on.

Rolling Over

Encourage your baby to roll from back to tummy by holding a toy just out of reach over baby's shoulder. As she turns to look at it, move the toy behind her head slowly. She may arch her back, lift her head with both hands extended, and flip herself over. You can help her get the feel for this by moving her arms in position and giving her a little nudge as she starts to roll to the side.

Materials: toy

Developing Skills
- gross motor coordination
- spatial awareness

Stand Up

Stand Up Song

(Sing to the tune of "Goodnight Ladies.")

Pull up baby, pull up baby

Pull up baby, pull up to a stand.

2nd verse

Stand up baby, stand up baby

Stand up baby, we're so glad you can.

Long before baby can walk, she will enjoy standing up. She strengthens her legs this way. Hold baby's hands and gently pull her up to a sitting position, then a standing position. She may want to remain standing for several minutes. What a great time to chat face-to-face.

Materials: none

Developing Skills

- gross motor coordination
- balance
- bilateral coordination

Crib Gym

Here is an easy toy to make for baby. Draw a face on the back of one paper plate. Glue foil to the back of a second plate. Staple the plates together around the perimeter so that the elastic fits through the middle of the plates. Tie one end of the elastic to each side of the crib. The baby should be able to kick at the plate and get it to spin. When baby can pull to a stand independently, this toy must be removed.

Materials: 3' (1 m) of 1/2"(1.3 cm) elastic, 2 paper plates, tin foil, glue, markers

Developing Skills

- eye-foot coordination
- lower-body strength
- visual tracking

Getting Ready to Crawl

Roll up a receiving blanket or a towel so its diameter is the same size as the length of baby's thigh. Now, place this roll under your baby's tummy so that the roll props up her middle. Now baby can actually feel the weight of her body on her knees. Place her toys in front of her and see if she can reach for them from this position.

This exercise helps build up the muscles in her thighs that she will need for crawling. Do this only as long as your child is comfortable. It is better to do this many times for short intervals than keep her in this position after she is unhappy. When both Mom and Dad are around, one parent can help maintain the baby's weight on her knees and the other can manipulate the toys to keep baby entertained.

Materials: blanket or towel, toys

Developing Skills

- spatial awareness
- upper and lower body strength
- coordination
- balance

Scoot, Scoot

When baby is on her tummy she will soon wave her arms and legs in an attempt to move by herself. Encourage her efforts by placing your palms against the bottoms of her feet. She will push off them. Push against her right foot, then her left foot, to encourage the alternating motion used in crawling. This works great on a smooth floor; she can scoot right along. Soon she'll be doing this on her own, especially with bare feet or non-slip socks for good traction.

Materials: none

Developing Skills

- gross motor coordination
- bilateral coordination

Are You Sleepy?

(Sing to the tune of "Are You Sleeping, Brother John?")

Are you sleepy? Are you sleepy?
Little one, little one,
Now it's time for naptime.
Now it's time for naptime.
Go to bed. Go to bed.

Additional last lines:

Rest your head. Rest your head.
Close your eyes. Close your eyes.
Have sweet dreams. Have sweet dreams.

Developing Skills

- bonding
- reinforcing routines
- exposure to music

The creeper is probably still not settled into a perfect nap routine. Make the most of what you have learned to calm your baby for a rest time. Does she like the blinds closed all the way or just halfway? Does she like a little background noise or does the room need to be quiet? You can help your baby find a routine by creating one. Try this song while patting baby on the back.

Materials: none

Developing Skills

- pre-verbal communication
- bonding
- self-awareness

Give 'em Five

Keeping a nap log allows you to notice the different stages of your baby's sleep. There is a period of sleep called *active sleep*, characterized by erratic movements of limbs, fluttering of eyelids, sucking, and rapid breathing. It is easy to misinterpret these signs as waking to feed. If your baby has doubled her birth weight, she may be ready to go 5–8 hours between feedings. Sleeping through the night may be possible now. When she rouses at night, try waiting her out. She could just be in active sleep. Wait five minutes before you go check on her. Remember, it is best to keep nighttime feedings as short as possible. Try to minimize interaction at this time, or she may look forward to these quiet nighttime meetings with you.

Materials: paper and writing implement

Kumbaya

Time for sleep now, Kumbaya.
Time for sleep now, Kumbaya.
Time for sleep now, Kumbaya.
Rest, rest, Kumbaya.

Additional verses:

Close your eyes now
Lay your head down
Mama/Papa loves you

Developing Skills

- reinforcing routines
- exposure to music
- bonding

This soothing song from the Congo originally had one word, *Kumbaya*, repeated throughout. Try this adaptation in your bedtime routine.

Materials: none

The Eyes Have It

Developing Skills

- trust
- pre-verbal communication
- cognitive development

Materials: none

Before your baby says a word, he will talk with his eyes. Because he does know so much more about his environment watch for this subtle method of communication.

His eyes say it all. Long before he can verbally ask you for something he can look at the object he wants. To enhance this communication, label things in the room and see if he looks for the object you named. As his eyes move to the object named say, "That's right, there's your ball." Then turn it around. Ask him what he wants, and see if he looks in the direction of a favorite toy. Follow his gaze and name the object at which he is staring. Offer it to him. This type of communication forms the building blocks of his first words.

Sign Language

Materials: none

Developing Skills

- pre-verbal communication
- fine motor coordination

Your baby is capable of learning some simple gestures to communicate long before he is able to say clear words. He probably is learning how to wave "bye-bye" already. The more consistently you use the American Sign Language (ASL) signs, the sooner baby will learn them. Baby's first attempts at repeating the signs may be months away. He needs many repetitions to make the association. Baby's lack of fine motor skills will only allow approximations of the exact movements. It's "baby talk" in sign language. Here are a few words to get you started.

To say the word *again*, in ASL, your right, cupped hand turns over so your fingertips land in your left, outstretched palm. (See illustration.) Use *again* when playing games. Sign as you say, "Let's do it again." or "Do you want to do it again? Let's read that book again."

Sign Language (cont.)

To say the word *help*, place your right fist on your left palm. Lift both hands together. Use the word *help* whenever you offer assistance to baby.

"I'll help you put your shirt on."

When baby fusses in frustration with a toy, sign as you say, "Do you want me to help you?"

To say the word *milk*, open and close your fist in a milking motion.

"Here is your milk."

Sign Language (cont.)

To say the word *more*, tap your fingertips together twice.

"Do you want more carrots?"

"Should we read another book?"

To say *done* or *all gone* hold your hands in front, palms facing toward each other. Quickly twist your wrists so your palms face downward.

"Are you finished with lunch."

"The crackers are all gone."

"Bath time is done."

Changing Table Chant

Diaper changes are a frequent occurrence and create a natural opportunity for repetition. Remember, one-on-one time is the best time to learn language. Naming body parts and describing what is coming next in the sequence of the change is an opportunity for cognitive growth. Your crawler can learn to associate words for body parts and anticipate what will be happening to him. Have your baby hold the dry diaper while you say this chant.

Materials: diapers, wipes

Developing Skills

- anticipation
- body awareness
- reinforcing routines

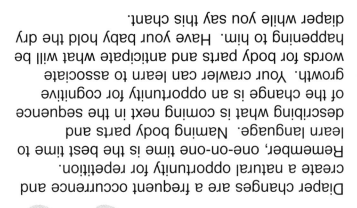

Changing Table Chant

Now it's time to change the diaper
Take off pants and get the wiper.
Make the baby nice and clean
Change to a dry one.

(Take dry diaper from baby.)

One, Two, Three!

(Quickly finish and swing baby down from the table to the floor on the count of three.)

Changing Table Mobile

One way to keep the diapering routine new and exciting is to create your own home-made mobile to place over the changing table. First cut out pictures from a magazine or use photos of family members. Mount them on small boxes so that they have a three dimensional look. Hang them by fishing line or ribbon from a padded hanger. Baby sees them from underneath so be sure it is interesting to look at from his point of view. Change these pictures once a week. Make sure they are objects or people with which baby is familiar. Replace the pictures from the previous week and see if baby remembers looking at them from before. This is a great way to reinforce first words.

Materials: several pictures cut from magazines or photos, small boxes, ribbon, and a hanger

Developing Skills

- visual memory
- language stimulation

Diddle Dumpling

Sometimes crawlers don't like to sit still while you dress them. Distract baby with this adapted nursery rhyme.

Diddle Diddle Dumpling

Diddle, diddle, dumpling, my son, John.

Time to put your trousers on.

One shoe off and one shoe on

Diddle, diddle, dumpling, my son, John.

Variation: Substitute your child's name. Change the second line to "Time to put your *shirt* on, time to put your *socks* on," etc.

Materials: clothing

Developing Skills

- reinforcing routines
- vocabulary enrichment
- pre-literacy skills

Cobbler, Cobbler

Here is another dressing rhyme to get you through putting shoes on. Particularly wiggly babies need the rhyme repeated a few times before both shoes are on.

Cobbler, Cobbler Mend My Shoe

Cobbler, cobbler, mend my shoe!
(Put one shoe on.)

Get it done by half past two.
(Fasten that shoe.)

Stitch it up and stitch it down.
(Tickle up and down baby's legs.)

You're the cutest baby in town.
(Repeat the rhyme for the other foot.)

Developing Skills

- reinforcing routines
- tactile stimulation
- pre-literacy skills

Enhancing Daily Routines

Crawlers

Snack Time Fun

Here is an activity that will help your crawler develop the fine motor ability to use a pincer grasp. It can also help a busy mom who needs a few minutes to work in the kitchen. Place the crawler in his high chair. Pour a small amount of maple syrup onto the tray. Add bits of cracker or o-shaped cereal to this syrup. The slight resistance that the syrup provides is just enough to help the crawler improve his pincer grasp as he tries to remove the treats. He's happy eating a snack and you have time to finish preparing supper!

Materials: maple syrup, crackers, o-shaped cereal

Developing Skills

- eye-hand coordination
- bilateral coordination
- fine motor coordination
- grasp and release

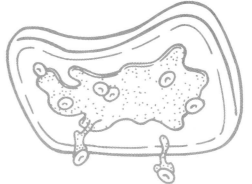

Toy Overboard

Tie a sturdy string around one of baby's toys. Tie the other end to his high chair. When he throws the toy "overboard," show him how to retrieve it himself by pulling up the string. Now he can experiment on his own. Keep the string short so that baby can't wrap it around his neck.

Materials: string, small toys

Developing Skills

- eye-hand coordination
- grasp and release
- problem solving

Ping-Pong Bath

Now that your baby can sit up, bath time becomes another opportunity to play. If baby still needs support for safety, try a seat designed for the tub. Move a Ping-Pong ball under the water and release it while you sing this song to the tune of "Pop Goes the Weasel."

All around the bath tub,
The baby chased the ball.
The baby thought it was all in fun,
POP goes the ball!

Encourage baby to experiment with a ball of his own. Watch your baby carefully to make sure he doesn't put the ball in his mouth.

Materials: Ping-Pong balls

Developing Skills

- visual tracking
- eye-hand coordination
- anticipation

Bath Time

This is the Way

This is the way we wash our toes,
Wash our toes, wash our toes.
This is the way we wash our toes
When we take our bath.

Additional Verses: Substitute different body parts for "toes."

Developing Skills

- tactile stimulation
- vocabulary enrichment
- body awareness

Bath time can be a learning time. Just think of all the language you use when doing this task. Describe actions, name body parts, and toys. The opportunities are endless. Here is a bath time tune that is fun to add to the routine event. Sing it to the tune of "Here We Go 'Round the Mulberry Bush."

Floating Ice Cubes

Add ice cubes to baby's bath water to give the sensory experience of cold. Tint the water with food coloring before freezing it to make the ice cubes more visible. Use rich language to enhance the activity. Vocabulary words include *cold, ice, wet, melt,* and *float.*

Variation: Make bigger ice cubes by freezing water in plastic cups or bowls. Freeze juice can lids within the ice.

Materials: ice cubes

Developing Skills

- visual tracking
- eye-hand coordination
- sensory stimulation

Where's the Lid?

Now that your baby can sit up it will be fun to modify the potato chip can toy (page 90). Take the plastic lid and cut a slot wide enough for the juice can lid to fit through. This changes the toy that had been used as a large muscle toy into one that can exercise the fine motor muscles. Show the baby how the lids can disappear through the slot and hide inside the can. The baby will not have enough strength to take off the plastic lid but he will enjoy having the lids disappear into the can. Keep saving those juice can lids. The next way that this toy can be modified requires lots of lids.

Materials: potato chip can toy (page 90); juice can lids

Developing Skills

- visual tracking
- grasp and release (pincer grasp)
- eye-hand coordination
- object permanence

Where's That Sound?

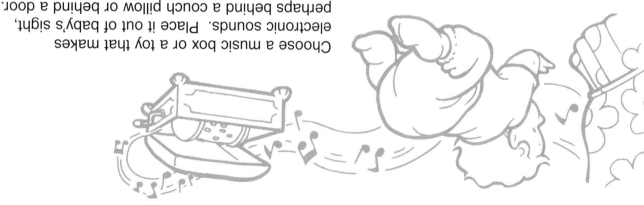

Choose a music box or a toy that makes electronic sounds. Place it out of baby's sight, perhaps behind a couch pillow or behind a door. Activate the sound and prompt baby to find it. "Did you hear that? Listen. Where is that sound coming from? Let's go find it!" Help baby locate the toy. Repeat the game. Soon baby will be looking without much help.

Materials: music box or toy that makes noise

Developing Skills

- auditory tracking
- gross motor play
- object permanence

Under the Scarf

In this game your baby will learn to find hidden toys. At first, partially cover the toy under one cloth. Once he can find the partially hidden toy, cover the toy completely. Next, switch the toy from one cloth to the other cloth. First, let him see you make the switch, then hide the switch. Progressing through these stages may take weeks. **Variation:** Use a piece of cardboard as a screen and see if your baby will look behind or over it to find a favorite toy.

Materials: 2 small 12" (30 cm) squares of cloth, one small toy

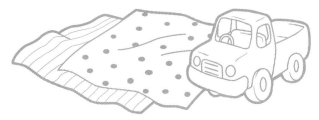

Developing Skills

- object permanence
- problem solving
- visual memory

Baby Wipes Boxes

Baby wipes boxes have all sorts of uses. At this age, a box makes a perfect object-permanence toy. While your baby is watching, put a favorite toy in the box. Prompt your baby to retrieve it. Show him where the toy is, if necessary. Repeat the process. Use words of encouragement. "Where did that toy go? Can you find it? Let's look in the box. Open the box. You can do it! There it is! You found it! Let's do it again."

Materials: baby wipes box, small toy

Developing Skills

- fine motor coordination
- object permanence
- vocabulary enrichment

Plastic Cups

Have several sizes of disposable cups available for baby. The cups nest and stack. Try these simple games.

- With your baby watching, hide a small toy under one of two cups. Ask, "Where did that toy go?" Does your baby look under the right cup? Try this "shell game" by exchanging the position of the cups.
- Show your baby how to pour a few large beads from one cup to the other and back again.
- Let baby use his hands to put small objects in and out of the cups.
- Stack six cups in a pyramid shape for your baby to knock down.

Materials: different-sized cups

Developing Skills

- object permanence
- fine motor coordination
- gross motor coordination
- spatial relationships

Tear It Up

Show your baby how to tear old magazines, waxpaper, newspaper, and paper towels. Grip a sheet with both hands and pull slowly and dramatically. Let baby try. You may have to get it started for him to overcome the initial resistance. Each kind of paper requires a different amount of "pull" and makes its own sound. Supervise your crawler. Don't let him put the scraps of paper in his mouth. (Wax paper doesn't "dissolve" as easily and is a little safer.)

Materials: newspapers and magazines; waxpaper; paper towels

Developing Skills

- grip strength
- fine motor coordination
- auditory stimulation

Toys on a String

Tie a sturdy string to one of baby's small toys. Put the toy in full sight, but out of reach, and show baby how to pull it toward him. Do this several times, putting the toy out of sight (under the couch, behind a door) some of the time. With the toy in sight, try cutting the string while baby is pulling it. Does he still pull on it or does he notice the tension is gone and retrieve the toy directly? This is a supervised activity. Do not let baby play with any kind of string alone. It poses a safety hazard.

Materials: small toys, string

Developing Skills

- object permanence
- fine motor skills
- problem solving

Through the Tube

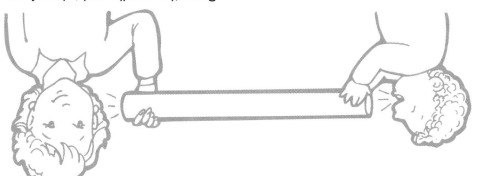

Save the cardboard tubes from paper towels. Your baby will find it intriguing to hear your voice as you talk through it. Encourage him to talk through it. Now look at your baby through the tube. Hold the tube up for him to look through. Again, he will delight in discovering you in a new way.

Materials: cardboard tubes

Developing Skills

- fine motor skills
- auditory stimulation
- visual stimulation

Picture Perfect

Developing Skills

- vocabulary enrichment
- social-emotional development

Help shape your baby's babbling into "mama" and "dada" with pictures of you. Have a good quality head shot, at least 3" x 5" (8 cm x 13 cm) of each of parent. Mount the pictures on sturdy cardboard and cover them with clear shelf paper. Let your baby hold one picture as you repeatedly say "mama." Later on, hold both pictures up and say "This is "Mama;" this is Dada." Try playing "Where is Daddy, Where is Mama?" and placing both pictures in front of baby. Let him point them out or hand them to you. Don't be surprised if your baby learns "Dada" first and calls any person, including Mom, by that name. That is typical.

Materials: photos of parents, clear shelf paper, cardboard

Criss Cross

Criss Cross Applesauce

Criss Cross
(Draw an X on baby's back.)

Applesauce
(Tap your fingers on his shoulders once for each syllable in "applesauce.")

Spiders crawling up your spine
(Walk and wiggle the fingers of both hands up his back.)

Cool breeze
(Gently blow on the back of his neck.)

Tight squeeze
(Give him a hug from behind.)

Now you've got the SHIVERS!
(Tickle baby.)

Developing Skills

- tactile stimulation
- anticipation

Now that your baby is sitting up well, try this activity on his back. Sit behind him.

Round the Sun

Sally Go Round the Sun

Sally go round the sun.

(Hold baby facing you and spin to the right.)

Sally go round the moon.

(Spin to the left.)

Sally go round the chimney tops,

(Spin to the right.)

Every afternoon!

(Spin to the left.)

Developing Skills

- balance
- spatial awareness
- vocabulary enrichment

Spinning stimulates the development of the vestibular system which controls our sense of balance. This rhyme is perfect for twirling.

Blanket Rides

Blanket Rides

Choo-choo-choo-choo,

Choo-choo-choo-choo,

Train's a-coming down the track.

Choo-choo-choo-choo,

Choo-choo-choo-choo,

Now the train is coming back.

Developing Skills

- balance
- torso strength
- vocabulary enrichment

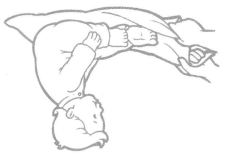

Help develop your baby's balance while sitting up by giving blanket rides. Sit baby on the center of a blanket on a smooth floor. Hold the edge of the blanket and walk slowly in a circle. Sing "Ring Around the Rosie" and drop the blanket on "all fall down." **Variation:** When baby is sturdier, he will enjoy being pulled all around the room. Say this train chant as you pull the blanket around.

Materials: blanket

Can You Find Me?

Now that the your baby is more mobile, he can get himself into positions where he can no longer see you. It is important to keep playing this game. Start with a scarf or cloth over baby's head. Say the chant.

Where is baby?

(Call the child's name.)

There you are.

(Let the baby pull the scarf off.)

Developing Skills

- object permanence
- self-awareness
- following a simple command

Where is Daddy?

Find me.

Here I am.

You found me!

Variation: It's fun to play this game with the scarf over Mommy or Daddy's face, because now the baby can pull the scarf off the parent's face to answer the chant.

Materials: scarf

Worm in the Apple

You can make a simple puppet using a light colored sock. Just draw a face on the sock and put it on your hand. Use your other hand to hide the sock or put the puppet behind a pillow or chair. Repeat the "Worm in the Apple" chant while manipulating the "worm" puppet. For added interest, cut a hole in a large apple cutout.

Materials: light colored sock, felt pen

Worm in the Apple

Worm in the apple
(Hide your puppet.)

Hiding so still.
Won't you come out?
(Begin to peek your puppet out.)

Yes I will!
(Pop out on cue!)

Developing Skills

- object permanence
- anticipation

Tambourine Time

Developing Skills

- gross motor coordination
- exposure to tempo and rhythm
- music appreciation

Now that baby knows how to hold and shake things, make her a tambourine to accompany the song "Jingle Bells" or the jingle rhymes on pages 84–86. Use a hole punch to make 16 holes spaced evenly around the edge of a plastic lid. Weave a sturdy cord or ribbon through the first hole. Slide a jingle bell down the cord before weaving it through the second hole. Come up through the third hole and add another bell before going through the fourth hole. Continue all the way around and tie off the ends of the cord securely. Make two or three more so the whole family can join in.

Materials: 8 jingle bells; a plastic coffee can lid; cord, ribbon or string

Caution: This toy should only be used with adult supervision. It should be stored out of baby's reach when not in use.

Throw the Ball

Sit facing a few feet away from your baby. Roll a small ball to him and prompt him to throw the ball back to you. "Throw it to Daddy/Mommy." Extend your hands and gesture to throw the ball, using a beckoning motion. As soon as baby drops the ball, clap and smile, and say, "Good throw!" Retrieve the ball and do it again. With repetition, you will shape your baby's behavior, and he will need much less prompting as he learns what "throw it" means.

Materials: ball

Developing Skills

- gross motor coordination
- following directions
- vocabulary enrichment

Crawling Challenge

Create ways for baby to expand his crawling abilities. Place pillows in his path so he has to climb over them to get to you. Make your body an obstacle. Lay on your side and encourage your baby to climb over you to get to his toy. Make a little tunnel by draping a blanket over two chairs. You may have to coax your baby from the other side to crawl through.

Materials: pillows, toy, blankets

Developing Skills

- gross motor coordination
- problem solving
- spatial awareness

Surprise Pictures

Place pictures within baby's range of sight to encourage crawling. Look through magazines for interesting pictures of children, animals, and objects that your baby recognizes. Tape those pictures inside of cupboard doors that you allow your child to open. Another spot is on the bottoms of kitchen or dining room chair seats. This way the pictures are not in the way of your normal décor. The baby finds it fascinating to see a picture of one of his favorite things as he goes crawling along. Protect the picture from tearing by covering it with clear shelf paper, leaving a ½ inch (1.3 cm) edge around the entire border. Change these pictures on a regular basis to include new words that your baby is learning.

Materials: magazine pictures, cellophane tape, shelf paper

Developing Skills

- vocabulary enrichment
- visual discrimination
- visual memory

Tug of War

Play this game on a carpeted surface. Give baby one end of a scarf or thick cord to hold. Gently pull the other end. When he pulls back, over-exaggerate his strength by falling forward. You will become a living "cause and effect" toy. Repeat the pulling, varying the tension on the rope to make baby adjust his balance. Let him pull you over again.

Variation: Sit on the left side of baby and have him pull with his right hand and vise versa to create a cross-the-midline activity.

Materials: a long scarf or thick rope

Developing Skills

- torso strength
- balance
- cross lateral movement

Baby in a Box

Use a large cardboard box or laundry basket for this whole body sensory activity. Fill the box half way with crumpled paper balls or paper from a paper shredder. Place baby in the box. Let him explore. Add a few small toys that he can hide and find in the paper.

Materials: large box or basket, shredded tissue paper, small toys

Developing Skills

- sensory motor play
- tactile stimulation
- object permanence

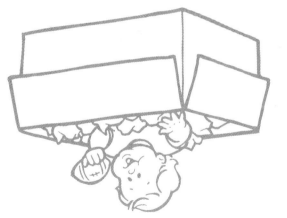

Up, Up and Away

Have two adults support baby. Gently swing him back and forth. Repeat the following chant as he swings.

Up, Up and Away

Up, up and away

Up, up and away

Up, up and away you GO!

Release your hold on "GO," gently dropping baby on a bed or similar cushioned surface.

Safety Hint: Never swing baby by the arms or hands. It puts too much stress on the shoulder joints.

Materials: none

Developing Skills

- balance
- spatial awareness

A Swinging Song

Sing to the tune of "It's Raining, It's Pouring."

A Swinging Song

You're swinging, you're swinging,

You're swinging in your swing.

You go up high and you come down low,

When you're swinging in you're swing,

Up high, down low,

Come again it's fun to swing.

Developing Skills

- balance
- spatial awareness
- vocabulary enrichment

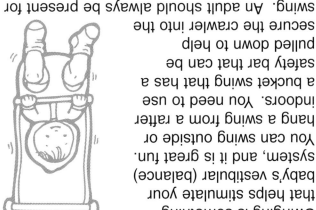

Swinging is something that helps stimulate your baby's vestibular (balance) system, and it is great fun. You can swing outside or hang a swing from a rafter indoors. You need to use a bucket swing that has a safety bar that can be pulled down to help secure the crawler into the swing. An adult should always be present for this activity.

Safety Hint: Indoor swings are great until the crawler starts walking. Then its time to secure the swing out of baby's reach when not in use. You don't want your little one to climb into the swing and try this by himself.

Cardboard Blocks

It's fun to have special toys just for outside. Make large cardboard blocks from half gallon paper milk cartons. You need two cartons for each block. Cut off the tops; and rinse the cartons well. After they have dried, insert the open end of one carton inside the other, to create a strong rectangle. Cover the block with shelf paper. It may take a while, but you can collect quite a set! These lightweight blocks are perfect for little ones to start stacking. When the blocks get knocked over on baby, it doesn't hurt. Find a large plastic crate for storage and keep it in the garage. Pull them outside for quick construction projects.

Materials: ½ gallon paper milk cartons, shelf paper

Developing Skills

- problem solving
- gross motor skills
- spatial awareness

Crib Mirror

By now your crawler may be able to pull up to a standing position. Keeping favorite toys in the crib may not be safe any longer. He could possibly stack them up, stand on them, and go over the side. It is better at this time to remove all toys from the crib.

Hang a mirror on the outside of the crib. Your crawler will enjoy looking at himself and you may hear him talking with his new friend in the mirror on those early mornings.

Materials: safety mirror

Developing Skills

- balance
- self awareness
- expressive language

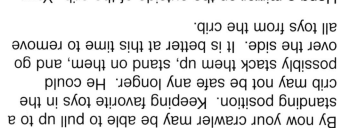

Good Night

The crawler is so busy throughout his day that it will be helpful to have a settling-in time before going in the crib. He is ready for a "good night" book. Choose a board book with only a few pages. A traditional favorite is *Good Night Moon* by Margaret Wise Brown.

After you read the text, you can make the circuit of his own bedroom saying good night to his toys and furniture. It will help to have a routine of turning the night light on, or any other ritual that baby has learned to expect. This makes bedtime predictable and helps the crawler anticipate the sequence of events and the expected behavior—sleep! Sweet dreams little one . . .

Materials: none

Developing Skills

- receptive language
- trust
- cognitive development

Introducing a "Lovey"

Separation anxiety typically begins between 9 months and 12 months of age. Baby, who willingly went to anyone, now will only accept comfort from Mom or Dad. This developmental milestone should be celebrated. It is a sign of baby's ability for visual memory. He now has a definite image of who the important people in his life are. No substitutes will do.

Now is the time to introduce a "lovey" object that represents comfort. This may be a blanket or small stuffed animal. Find something that the crawler can take with him when his important people are away. Be observant. Your baby may prefer certain textures or fabrics. Even a plastic car can serve as a "lovey" if he refuses something cuddly. After all, it is the baby's choice of what he has grown attached to that will help with transitions of separation.

Developing Skills

- cognitive development
- social development
- trust

Back to Sleep

It is common for the crawler to have some disruption of his nighttime sleep patterns. He is so busy during the day working on motor skills that he can't "turn it off" at night. It is common to find your crawler standing up in the crib, hanging on for dear life because he pulled up to a stand and can't get back down.

It is really important for you to have a plan of how you want to deal with this night waking. The quiet calmness of the night can invite the crawler to want to engage in social interaction. If you can refrain from picking him up your chances will be greater of getting him back to sleep. So just go in, rub his back, and say very quietly, "It's dark outside, we're all asleep. It's time for you to go to sleep."

Developing Skills

- trust
- social skills

I'll Be Back

Your cruiser will cry when you walk out of the room, even if she was playing contentedly without you. It is more than object permanence. Her growing cognitive ability makes her aware that you and she are separate beings and that she cannot control your movement. This separation anxiety is part of normal development. Before you leave the room, tell her where you are going. Explain that you will come back. "I'm going to put a load of laundry in. I'll be right back." Continue to talk if that voice contact reassures her. Purposely leave for short periods, returning with, "See, I came back. I always come back." It is only through her repeated experience of your leaving and returning that she learns to trust that you will come back and that she is okay without you for a while.

Materials: none

Developing Skills

- social-emotional development
- trust

Look Who's Pointing

Baby is on the move! Her world is increasing and she has discovered that she can do something that gets mom's and dad's attention. She can point! With one little movement of her finger, mom and dad can follow her point and bring the world to her. The sense of power is almost intoxicating.

Learning to point follows a sequence. Your baby learns it from you. At first, she looks at your finger, not at the object to which you are pointing. Before long, she starts to look where you point. Babies can begin to point as early as six months but they don't necessarily connect pointing with getting something until later. This skill of pointing is a developmental milestone and this is another step in expressive communication.

Developing Skills

- trust
- pre-verbal communication
- problem solving

Changing Table Mirror

The cruiser's most important developmental skill involves moving, so tasks that require her to be still become far more challenging. The changing table mobile may become more distracting than helpful. Most likely, the cruiser will try to reach for the mobile and make it move because she has the ability to remember and a knowledge of cause-and-effect thinking.

Replace the mobile with a mirror placed on the wall alongside the changing table. The cruiser will enjoy looking at her image. She will also like to point out body parts on the mirror. You can help focus her on the task at hand by continuing to sing the changing table chant and song from pages 62 and 104.

Materials: safety mirror

Developing Skills

- language stimulation
- spatial awareness
- social skills

Bucket of Toys

Assemble a small bucket of toys and store it near the changing table. Books or small manipulative toys work best. Change these toys frequently. It is the novelty and the surprise that keep baby preoccupied and interested.

As you sing a diaper-changing song it helps remind her what is coming next. Make a stop at the special bucket and let her choose something to play with while you change her. Never stop talking about what is actually going on. This language-building experience is important for her to add to her vocabulary (body parts, wet, dry, messy, clean) and it helps her to know when she can anticipate being finished. The more you talk, the more she can be engaged in what is happening.

Materials: small bucket of toys

Developing Skills

- body awareness
- vocabulary enrichment
- tactile stimulation

Dressing

Your cruiser is so excited about moving around that standing still to be dressed becomes quite a challenge. Again, having a song to sing as part of the routine can help her anticipate what is coming next and help her remember what behavior is expected. Listening to the song distracts her from moving—at least momentarily. The same song you sing when you take a bath can now help her put on her clothes.

Developing Skills

- vocabulary enrichment
- bilateral coordination
- following directions

Getting Dressed Song

(Sing to the tune of "Here We Go 'Round the Mulberry Bush.")

This is the way we put on our shirt,
Put on our shirt, put on our shirt.
This is the way we put on our shirt
When we get dressed in the morning.

Additional Verses: Substitute the item of clothing that needs to go on next.

Kitchen Fun

Store 3–5 small, square blocks in one of the kitchen drawers. The blocks are going to help you teach your cruiser preposition words (spatial concepts). Take out a plastic cup and ask your cruiser to put her blocks *into* the cup, *under* the cup, *on* the cup, *out* of the cup. This is a good high chair time game. If she plays on her own, without following your directions, simply narrate what she is doing with the blocks. "Now you poured them *out*. I see one block *in* the cup."

Variation: Build towers with these small blocks at another time to talk about *on* and *under*.

Materials: small blocks or other small toys, cup

Developing Skills

- problem solving
- spatial awareness
- grasp and release

Mealtime Madness

Babies always want to eat before the meal is ready. Prepare a special toy that you store in the kitchen to help with the "mealtime madness." Use a small box with a hinged lid (cigar box or jewelry box) that your cruiser can easily lift open. Store a small, clear plastic pill bottle (no lid) inside the box. Put some cereal into the bottle and see if she can get the cereal by opening the box and turning the bottle over by rotating her forearm. Give her other small objects to hide in her box with the lid. This can keep her busy while you finish supper.

Variation: You can also use a small, clear baby formula bottle. The attraction for the cruiser is that she can see that there is something inside the bottle that she needs to turn over to dump out.

Materials: small plastic bottle, cigar box or other hinged box, small toys or cereal

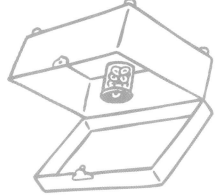

Developing Skills

- grasp and release
- fine motor skills
- problem solving

Dipping

Your cruiser will love dipping her food. This helps her to define her pincer grasp. She will be able to use just her thumb and pointer finger for this fine motor activity. First, try small pieces of soft bread or tiny crackers that can be dunked in a dip. Favorite first dips include ketchup, yogurt, and soft cream cheese. Try these recipes for an added treat. Just mix and eat!

Sweet Fruit Dip

1 jar marshmallow cream (10 oz)

8 oz. cream cheese (softened)

2 Tbls. orange juice concentrate

Tangy Vegetable Dip

1 cup plain yogurt

1 cup mayonnaise

1 pkg. ranch dressing

Developing Skills

- fine motor skills
- grasp and release
- eye-hand coordination

Tub Toys

Developing Skills

- sensory motor play
- problem solving

Include household items in the tub to promote experimentation and discovery. Try plastic funnels, small cups, small sieves, little scoops (from formula cans and powdered laundry detergent), and plastic water bottles with squirt tops. Your baby will gain knowledge about squeezing and pouring, empty and full, more and less, float and sink, etc.

Materials: plastic funnels, small cups, small sieves, little scoops, plastic water bottles with squirt tops.

Washing Dolly

Let your cruiser bring a "friend" in the tub with her. A plastic baby doll provides many opportunities to learn. Give your cruiser a little sponge or small washcloth. Tell her to wash her baby's legs. Now wash your baby's arms. You can take turns. The adult washes a body part on the child and then the child washes the same part on the doll. It is also fun to free play with the doll so your cruiser is deciding what to do next.

Materials: baby doll, wash cloth

Developing Skills

- fine motor coordination
- vocabulary: body part identification
- receptive language: following directions

Enhancing Daily Routines

Cruisers

Same and Different

Use a large potato chip can and some juice can lids. Purchase stickers of simple items that represent words baby knows, such as animal names. Place the stickers on the indented sides of the lids. If your baby still puts most things in her mouth, cover the sticker with clear shelf paper to make it more secure.

Have baby find the lids that have certain animals, like dogs, and make them disappear into the can. Now find another animal. You can also talk about *same* and *different*.

Variation: Practice making animal sounds when you look at what animal is on the lid. Make the sound first and baby will imitate it.

Materials: large potato chip or baby formula can, juice can lids, stickers, clear shelf paper

Developing Skills

- vocabulary enrichment
- following directions
- problem solving
- visual discrimination

Pat Mat

While your cruiser is standing at the coffee table, let her pat, poke, and squish at this homemade toy. Make two different colors (flavors) of gelatin dessert. Put some of each color in a large resealable plastic storage bag. Show baby how to poke and pat it. Watch the colors mix. If you don't want baby to be able to pick it up, duct tape the bag to a cookie sheet first.

Materials: gelatin (2 different colors), large resealable bag (optional: duct tape, cookie sheet)

Developing Skills

- balance
- leg strength
- visual discrimination of color

First Sand Box

Cruisers like to empty and fill things. One way to extend a time of sitting quietly is to make a highchair sensory play box. Use a plastic shoe box (the kind that has a snap-on lid). Fill it with about two cups of corn meal. Keep the scoops from formula cans and the lids to deodorant cans and fabric softeners, or various other cup-like-lids that are small. This becomes a first kind of sand box. The cruiser can fill and empty the small cups. If she eats the "sand," it won't hurt her. Restricting this activity to the high chair helps baby learn that the "sand" stays in the box.

Materials: plastic container with a lid, corn meal, scoops

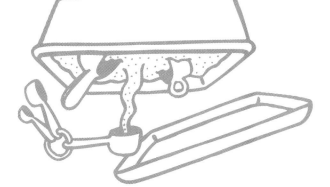

Developing Skills

- problem solving
- grasp and release
- tactile stimulation

Messy Mirror

Place an unbreakable mirror on baby's high chair tray. Put a dollop of pudding or yogurt on the mirror. You don't have to encourage baby to take a taste. (Use something edible to keep it non-toxic.) Show baby how to smear the goop all around the smooth surface. She will see her reflection appear, and disappear, and will explore the tactile sensations.

Materials: unbreakable mirror, pudding or yogurt

Developing Skills

- sensory motor play
- tactile stimulation
- self-awareness

Find Teddy's Nose

Babies know and understand many words before they can actually say them. Play games that give baby a chance to show her receptive skills. Give simple commands like "Show me Teddy's nose. Where is your nose? Where is Mommy's nose?" Keep playing, substituting other body parts.

Variation: Place a few familiar objects in front of baby. Ask her to give you different items. "Give me the book. Give me the cup. Give me the ball." If she hands you the book, when you asked for the ball just reinforce what she gave you: "This is a book. You gave me a book. Where is the ball?"

Materials: Teddy bear

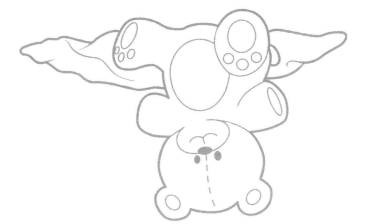

Developing Skills

- receptive language
- vocabulary enrichment
- following directions

Touch and Feel Box

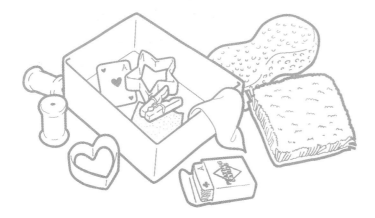

Cruisers like to explore containers by dumping and refilling them. Put a variety of unusual items in a shoebox for her to explore. Pay attention to the textures. Remember, one important way your baby explores is by feeling things with her mouth. Make sure the objects are large so that she does not choke. Change the items frequently to renew interest. This is a great opportunity to introduce texture words like *smooth, scratchy, rough, soft, bumpy, furry,* etc.

Materials: shoe box, various toys and household objects

Suggestions: a sponge, plastic cookie cutters, fabric scraps like corduroy and satin, a carpet swatch, sandpaper, a spool, a plastic coated playing card, a clothespin.

Developing Skills

- fine motor coordination
- tactile stimulation

Hats Off to You

Introduce your baby to pretend play. Dress up with hats, wigs, and plastic sunglasses. The two of you can try on a variety of them in front of a mirror. Baby will watch you change into someone else. She will probably be surprised when you remove your disguise and your familiar image returns. Encourage her to watch herself in the mirror. It takes a special combination of object permanence and self-awareness to realize that you don't change into someone else. It's just you (or Mom or Dad) with a costume on.

Materials: dress up clothes and accessories

Developing Skills

- fine motor coordination
- self-awareness
- object permanence

Blowing Bubbles

Developing Skills

- visual tracking
- eye-hand coordination
- fine motor coordination

Invest in a small bottle of bubbles or make your own with diluted dish soap or baby shampoo. Make bubble wands from chenille sticks. Blow bubbles for baby to watch and try to catch. She will be fascinated by the way the bubbles float, drift, and pop when she touches them. If it isn't too windy, try this outside too.

Materials: bubbles, wand or chenille stick

Wrap It Up

Hide some of baby's favorite toys for her to find. Wrap one in a dishtowel, some tissue paper, or a piece of newspaper. You don't need tape or ribbon. Have your baby watch you wrap up her toy. See if she will spontaneously unwrap it when you put it down. Show her where the toy "went," if you need to. After some practice, give her the toy already wrapped and see if she remembers how to find it.

Materials: small toys, a towel, tissue paper or newspaper

Developing Skills

- object permanence
- problem-solving
- fine motor coordination

Use Your Finger

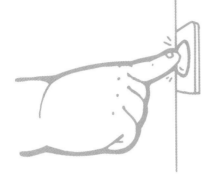

Let baby do some "grown-up" things like turn off the light switch or push the elevator button. She will feel proud of herself and isolate the use of her index finger as a useful tool. Other ideas include ringing a doorbell, pushing a microwave button, tapping on a keyboard, and pushing buttons on an old telephone. Your baby will like using real things instead of toy versions. This mimicking adult behavior will turn into pretend play someday.

Materials: none

Developing Skills

- cause and effect
- problem-solving
- fine motor coordination

Toe Touch Game

Begin with you and baby sitting on the floor facing each other. Baby's legs should be outstretched and slightly apart. Hold her right hand and don't let it go. Place a plastic cup over her right foot and encourage her to remove it with her left hand. Repeat a few times. Now switch: hold her left hand, put the cup on her left foot and encourage her to remove it with her right hand. This game gives your baby practice crossing the midline of her body. This ability is necessary to develop reading skills. The eyes must cross the midline repeatedly as they scan from the left side of the page to the right side of the page. **Variation:** Play this game while changing diapers or getting dressed. Offer toys from the side so she has to reach across her midline to grab the toy.

Materials: a plastic cup

Developing Skills

- spatial awareness
- bilateral coordination
- cross lateral coordination

On/Off Day

On/Off Day

"Your diaper is *on*; now it's *off*."

"The TV is *on*; now it is *off*."

"Let's put your coat *on*."

"The teddy is *on* the bed; now he's *off*."

Variations: Make tomorrow In/Out Day or Up/Down Day.

Developing Skills

- conceptual thinking
- vocabulary enrichment

Help yourself and your baby focus on one concept at a time. Make today "On/Off Day." Point out this concept all day. Highlight and repeat the words whenever you can. Turn a light switch on and off as you say "on, off." Have "On/Off Day" again next week.

Materials: none

Find Me

This is a whole body version of the ever-popular peek-a-boo game. Object permanence is still not fully developed in children at this age. When you walk out of the room the child will cry because she thinks you have disappeared.

Hide behind a couch, under a table, or behind a door. Repeatedly call out, "Where am I? Come find me. Where did I go?" to give baby a sound to track. Peek out from your hiding place to help baby locate you if necessary. Show great animation and delight when she discovers you. The reunion is so sweet with an added hug and kiss. Tell baby, "I'm going to hide in the living room. Come find me."

Materials: none

Developing Skills

- object permanence
- auditory tracking
- vocabulary enrichment

Jack in the Box

Jack in the Box

Jack in the box, sitting so still

(Crouch down with hands on your head.)

Won't you come out? Yes I will!

(Pop up with arms lifted above your head.)

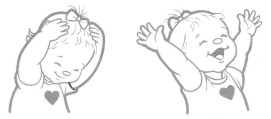

Demonstrate this body rhyme for baby. Soon she will imitate you. It is fun to do it together. Later, she will be able to do it by herself while you accompany her with the words only.

Materials: none

Developing Skills

- balance
- standing
- anticipation

Hammer Song

Hammer Song

Tap and pound, tap and pound,
Hammer all day long.
Tap and pound, tap and pound,
As we sing this song.
Tap and pound, tap and pound,
I love to tap along.
Tap and pound, tap and pound,
As we sing this song.

Developing Skills

- fine motor coordination
- imitation
- rhythm

Materials: two small blocks

Give baby two small blocks to bang together. Wooden blocks make a particularly appropriate sound. Tap in rhythm as you sing this song to the tune of "Jingle Bells."

Clap Your Hands

Cruisers can imitate simple gestures and movements. You may put your hands over your baby's and guide her through the motions at first. It will take many repetitions before a cruiser can follow along independently. Try two verses at first. Add the others one at a time as baby learns them.

Materials: none

Developing Skills

- fine motor coordination
- tempo
- following directions

Clap Your Hands

Clap, clap, clap your hands as slowly as you can.

(Face baby and demonstrate the motion slowly.)

Clap, clap, clap your hands as quickly as you can.

(Face baby and demonstrate the motion quickly.)

Additional verses:

- **Shake your hands**
- **Roll your hands**
- **Rub your hands**
- **Kick your feet**
- **Stomp your feet**

First Walker

Store-bought, "walk-behind" toys have wheels that often slip away from baby as she leans on them for support. Invert a plastic laundry basket for baby to push on carpeting. It won't tip over, and she can lean on it safely.

Materials: plastic laundry basket

Developing Skills

- gross motor coordination
- balance
- walking

After your cruiser is comfortable supporting her weight by holding on to a piece of furniture, stand her next to a wall so she can lean for support. First, try this facing the wall so she can put both hands on it. Then, try turning her sideways so only one hand is touching the wall for support. Now, offer her a toy. Will she stand and hold something? Will she stoop to pick up a toy placed on the floor near her?

Materials: toy

Developing Skills

- gross motor coordination
- balance
- walking

Active Play

Cruisers

Safe Stairs

Cruisers love to climb on the stairs. For safety, it is important to block access to the stairs with baby gates. However, you can place the gate on the third or fourth step from the bottom. This gives baby a few steps on which to safely practice climbing up and down. This idea is especially well suited for a carpeted landing and stairway.

Materials: baby gate, access to stairs

Developing Skills

- gross motor coordination
- balance

Wheelbarrow

This activity helps strengthen the muscles of the upper body. Lay baby on the floor, face down. Lift up her back end by holding around her upper thighs. Encourage her to walk with her hands. As she gets stronger, hold around her knees instead. This requires her to support more of her weight and still keep her back straight. Finally, progress to holding her just by the ankles.

Materials: none

Developing Skills

- balance
- bilateral coordination
- gross motor coordination

Just Cruisin'

A favorite activity at this stage is cruising around furniture. Baby proofing your house becomes critical. It will save you energy and worry if your house is a safe place for your cruiser to move around. It helps to get down on your knees and make the rounds. What is at your eye level now? Everything needs to be covered or somehow secured from cruiser's inquiring mind and grasp. Here is a fun song to sing while she is covering ground.

Materials: none

Developing Skills

- balance
- bilateral coordination
- gross motor coordination

Get Around Song
(Sing to the tune of the "Wheels on the Bus.")

The baby in the room goes
Walk, walk, walk
Walk, walk, walk,
Walk, walk, walk
The baby in the room goes
Walk, walk, walk
All around the furniture.

(Repeat)

Pulling Song

(Sing to the tune of "Mary Had a Little Lamb.")

Baby likes to pull her box,

Pull her box, pull her box.

Baby likes to pull her box,

All across the room.

Variation: Sing "Baby likes to push her box."

Developing Skills

- balance
- bilateral coordination
- gross motor coordination

Once baby can walk, she will love to push and pull things. Let her give her stuffed animals a ride. Supply her with a box or a laundry basket and watch the fun begin. Loop a belt or scarf through a hole in the basket to create a short handle. (Avoid long strings. They pose a strangulation hazard.) At first, the cruiser can only pull the toy walking backwards. With practice, she will go in both directions. Make sure that doors are closed and the stairways are blocked off during the ride. Sing the "Pulling Song" as you play.

Materials: box or laundry basket and stuffed animals

Balloon Batting

Balloons move slowly enough to let your baby practice the skills she will need for throwing and catching. Start with baby seated on the floor. Drop an inflated balloon from over your baby's head for her to catch. She may like just watching it fall at first. Show her how to bat at it, catch it, and throw it. Always supervise this activity.

Caution: Balloons that are not inflated, or popped balloon pieces, are a serious choking hazard.

Materials: balloon

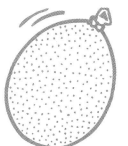

Developing Skills

- visual tracking
- eye-hand coordination
- gross motor coordination

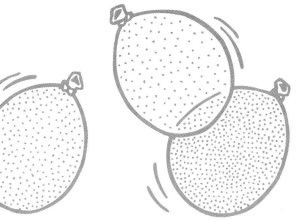

Ramps and Tubes

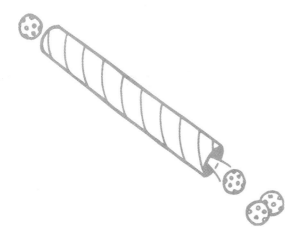

Let your cruiser experiment and problem solve with these simple set-ups. Show her how to roll golf balls down an empty wrapping paper tube or mailing tube. She won't expect them to come out the other end at first. Soon she will connect the cause and effect.

Make a ramp with a piece of stiff cardboard leaned against the couch. Roll balls and little vehicles down the ramp. What happens when you try to roll a stuffed animal or block down the ramp?

Materials: cardboard tubes, golf balls, a cardboard ramp, assorted toys

Developing Skills

- problem solving
- cause and effect
- fine motor coordination

Texture Blocks

Glue fabric scraps over small boxes to create different textures on different sides. Try corduroy, fake fur, different grades of sand paper, Mylar®, corrugated cardboard, etc. Make several, so baby can stack the blocks and topple them. Single serving cereal boxes, small milk cartons, and small jewelry boxes work well.

Materials: small boxes, fabric scraps, textured materials

Developing Skills

- fine motor coordination
- tactile stimulation

Spindle Toy

Developing Skills

- problem solving
- fine motor skills
- spatial awareness

Add this toy to your outside collection. It will last longer if it is covered with shelf paper. Cover the coffee can with one color paper. Cover the paper towel tube with a different color paper. Cut a hole in the plastic lid just large enough to slide the tube down into the can. Cut the inside circles out of six plastic plates to create rings. Now your cruiser can place the rings on the spindle in the can.

Materials: a coffee can or a formula can with a plastic lid, a paper towel or wrapping paper tube, 6 plastic-coated paper plates, shelf paper (two different colors)

Monster Rocking

This game encourages standing unaided and eventually walking alone. Stand your cruiser up, facing you. Hold both of her hands. Rock from side to side, lifting each foot off the ground as you shift your weight. (Remember how a mummy walks?) Try to get her to copy your movements. Add a silly sound like the "mummy" would make to entice her to imitate you. After she has been rocking back and forth holding your hands, see if she will take steps if you slowly pull her forward. Progress to walking alone with her hands held out in front of her. Cruisers need to practice walking and holding their arms out away from their bodies to help their balance.

Materials: none

Developing Skills

- bilateral coordination
- body awareness
- balance

Knee Walking

Set out two boxes or laundry baskets on the lawn. Fill one box with familiar toys. Now entice your little one to imitate you transferring the toys from the filled box to the empty box. Walk on your knees and carry each toy from one box to the other. A pre-walking child will enjoy the challenge. See how far she can make it across the grass before she goes back to crawling. At first the boxes will need to be fairly close together. Place the boxes farther apart as her travelling skills progress.

Materials: two boxes or baskets, one filled with toys

Developing Skills

- bilateral coordination
- balance
- lower-body strength

Bedtime Stories

Bedtime becomes a magic time once this pre-verbal baby gift of pointing as you read pictures books you are really engaging in a powerful literacy skill. The common bedtime scene of a good night book is rich in language stimulation and opportunity. One of the ways parents can help their children learn is by reading books and "labeling" the pictures in them. Research shows that it is never too early to reap the benefits of reading to children. The very fact that your baby can turn pages and look for pictures in a book sets the stage for reading skills to come. The findings from many studies are clear. The stage gets set for reading achievement for your child during infancy and the preschool years. What children learn about words as toddlers relates to later school performance.

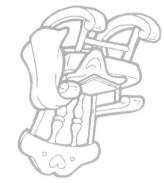

That bedtime story is more important than you may have thought. Reading provides an important route for vocabulary learning—a route that gives parent and child a great deal of pleasure. Go ahead and climb into the rocking chair. Read your favorite good night story aloud one more time. Remember, as you have your baby find and point to the pictures of the words you read, you are really getting her ready for school some day!

Expanding Bedtime

As baby grows older you will want to change some of the things she associates with sleep. Maybe you want to wean her from the breast or bottle. Introduce some other elements, one at a time, to the bedtime routine to help your cruiser transition from her active day to settling down for sleep. She can have a bedtime snack instead of her bottle if you feel she is ready. Serve the formula or milk in a cup with a nighttime cracker to ensure she has a full tummy. Perhaps you will introduce brushing teeth or cleaning up her room. Putting her stuffed animals to bed will help build her imagination with pretend play. When you add to a routine, your child builds memory, learns to sequence, and anticipates what happens next. Children learn through repetition. The more consistent you are with following the known sequence, the easier and more reassuring bedtime becomes.

Materials: none

Developing Skills

- reinforcing routines
- social-emotional development
- cognitive development

Tantrum Tamer

As climbers make gains in cognitive abilities, they are capable of more complex thoughts and ideas. They now have wants in addition to needs. Often they can't convey the details to you with their limited language. This is a common source of frustration. Climbers do not yet understand that while they will get everything they need, they won't get everything they want. Tantrums develop when climbers are overwhelmed by feelings of anger, disappointment, and lack of control. Try helping your child calm down by telling him to "blow Mommy's hair" while holding him in your arms. This creates a deep breathing exercise that helps your baby regain control. Practice blowing as a game so he has the skill when he needs it. Use the "Jeremiah Blow the Fire" rhyme from page 16 when you do this calming activity.

Materials: none

Developing Skills

- emotional awareness
- self control

The Angry Dance

Most human social and emotional behavior is learned. That means someone who has the skills has to model the behavior for us. Be your baby's emotions coach. Give him acceptable alternatives to hitting or biting out of anger. Let him stamp his feet in an "Angry Dance." Prompt him with words that accept his feelings but redirect his behavior. "No hitting. Let's stamp our feet to get those angry feelings out. You look angry enough to bite something. Let's go pound on the couch cushions instead." Just like every other type of learning, behavior skills take lots of repetition and reinforcement before they are mastered.

Materials: none

Developing Skills

- emotional awareness
- vocabulary: names of feelings
- self control

182

Sign Language: Feelings

Help your climber become aware and recognize his feelings. This step is necessary before learning to express feelings appropriately and to control them. Babies can learn gestures to represent feelings. Use these signs whenever you name a feeling of yours or your

Happy: Pat your chest with a slight upward motion a few times using an open hand shape.

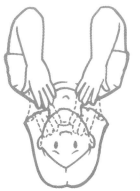

Sad: Use the "FIVE" hand shape. Start with hands in front of your face. Drop them slightly.

Developing Skills

- emotional awareness
- self control
- fine motor skills

Angry: Bend and unbend the fingers of one hand several times in front of your face.

Frustrated: The back of one open hand moves quickly toward your face.

Developing Skills

- emotional awareness
- self control

Materials: none

One Noun, One Verb

In general, use rich complete sentences when talking to your baby. He will learn vocabulary and sentence structure through repeated exposure. However, use one verb and one noun when you want to convey important limits or commands. When you say, "Don't kick your chair," your baby processes *kick* and *chair*. State your commands with the verb that represents what you want your climber to do. The simpler and more direct your statement is, the less interpretation is necessary.

Instead of "No running" or "Be careful," try saying "Walk now." Instead of "Can you help Mommy and stop squirming so I can change your diaper?" try saying "Lie down" or "Hold still."

Developing Skills

- understanding limits
- receptive language

Materials: none

Clean Up Time

Clean Up Time

Clean, clean, clean your room
Let's put things away
Books go on the bookshelf
Until another day.
Clean, clean, clean your room
We put everything away
Well done, give a cheer
Hurray, hurray, hurray!

Developing Skills

- vocabulary enrichment
- following directions
- self-help skills

Include your climber in your daily clean-up routine. He will learn by imitating you. This song gives specific, concrete directions that are easier to understand than broad statements like "clean this up." Sing to the tune "Row, Row, Row your Boat."

Additional verses: Change the third line to match the task: Clothes go in the hamper. Blocks go in the block box. Toys go in the basket.

Materials: things to clean up

Bathroom Diaper Changing

Climbers are so mobile. Rather than risk climbing up on a high changing table, switch to changing in the bathroom. Use a small portable changing surface and store your diapers and wipes in the bathroom. Climbers have tripled in size. Save your back and invite him to lie on top of the changing pad. You can kneel on the floor alongside your climber and do the change. Shake any solid matter in to the toilet. "This is where it goes." Let your climber flush. This is a good predecessor to potty training. Your climber will be used to going into the bathroom to care for his toileting needs.

Keep the climber engaged in what is happening. Talk about what you are doing throughout the changing process.

Developing Skills

- body awareness
- social development
- language stimulation

Shower Time

Climbers do not enjoy sitting down. Perhaps your climber would like changing from a bath to a shower. A hand-held shower nozzle is ideal for this transition. The water spray is a new tactile sensation. It is important to put a no slip pad in your shower for safety, and a bucket of toys for fun. Punch a few holes in the bottom of the bucket to let the water drain out. You will need to take your shower together, but in a busy world, this can become a time saver.

Materials: shower or shower nozzle

Developing Skills

- tactile stimulation
- trust
- body awareness

Brushing Teeth

Children cooperate better if you can make a game out of new routines. Try these suggestions if you need something to make teeth brushing easier.

- Let your climber choose between two brushes. "Do you want the red one or the blue one today?"
- Play "my turn, your turn." Alternate several times during brushing by announcing, "My turn." A few moments later, switch to "Your turn."
- Make "vroom, vroom" sounds and say "stop" and "go" as you drive around baby's mouth.
- Play "chase the germs." Tell baby you have to "Get that germ. Open wide. There goes another one. Got him! Oops, there's another germ. Let's get him."
- Use a washcloth instead of a toothbrush.

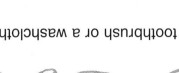

Materials: toothbrush or a washcloth

Developing Skills

- reinforcing routines
- self-help skills
- cooperation

Preposition Play

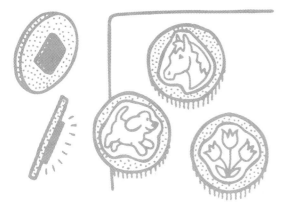

Find that potato chip can one more time. Change the juice lids with stickers to make this a refrigerator game. Place 1–2 inch (3–5 cm) pieces of magnetic stripping on the back of the juice lids. Now your lids will stick to the refrigerator door.

To play this game, ask your baby to "Put the doggie above the kitty" or "Put the fish below the kitty" or "Put the bird between the fish and the dog." The variations are endless and having your child demonstrate the prepositional words will help him in his future language skills.

Materials: potato chip can and lids (page 150), self-adhesive magnetic stripping (purchased by the foot at a fabric or hardware store)

Developing Skills

- visual memory
- bilateral coordination
- following directions
- spatial awareness

Slip and Slide

Tape a piece of bubble wrap on your baby's high chair tray. Spread on a thin layer of cooking oil, water, or lotion. Let baby smear his hands around on the bumpy, billowy surface. Use rich language: *slippery, bumpy, slick, slide.*

Caution: Always remove the bubble wrap immediately when finished. Never let baby handle or chew on any type of plastic wrap to avoid a suffocation or choking hazard.

Materials: bubble wrap, wide masking tape, cooking oil, water or lotion

Developing Skills

- fine motor coordination
- tactile stimulation
- vocabulary enrichment

Sensory Table Box

Climbers love to dump and fill and dump again. Provide an acceptable area for this play by creating a sensory table. Use a plastic "under the bed" storage box with a top. Place a vinyl tablecloth under the box to define the play space. Fill the box about one-inch high with uncooked oatmeal. Collect scoops, small containers, and a dump truck to fill up and dump out. A funnel wheel is also a good investment. It will take constant vigilance to help your climber learn to remain by the box. If he moves off the tablecloth, take his toys out of his hands and redirect him back to the box to continue to play. For quick clean up, shake the spilled grain outside. **Variations:** Use puffed rice cereal, grits, uncooked rice, or dried lentils in the box.

Materials: storage box, sand toys, vinyl tablecloth or shower curtain, oatmeal

Developing Skills

- tactile discrimination
- sensory exploration
- fine motor coordination
- spatial relationships

Water Play

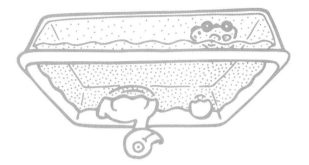

Climbers are fascinated with water. Use your sensory table (see previous page) to give baby an opportunity for water play outside the bathtub. Fill the box with an inch or two of warm water. Add food coloring to make the water easier to see. Let baby experiment with objects that sink or float. Use toy boats, Ping-Pong balls, practice golf balls, funnels, cups, tiny pitchers, and small sponges. Baby can catch objects in a goldfish net. Vary the toys available to renew interest. Model appropriate play by pouring and scooping in the box. Of course, your baby will get wet. If his play becomes too vigorous, put the top on and say "All done." After some repetition, he may come to understand the limits.

Materials: storage box, water toys, vinyl tablecloth or shower curtain

Developing Skills

- tactile discrimination
- sensory exploration
- fine motor coordination
- spatial relationships

Tabletop Bowling

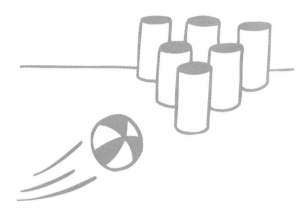

Stand the toilet paper rolls up in a 3, 2,1 pattern at one end of a coffee table or other low table. Show your climber how to roll the ball to knock down the "pins." Replace the pins and let your climber have a turn. After his turn, replace the pins for him. Soon he may want to set the pins up himself. It doesn't matter how he sets them up. He will like doing it himself.

Variation: If your climber will sit, play this game on the kitchen table.

Materials: 6 empty toilet paper tubes, a Ping-Pong ball or a small, soft indoor ball

Developing Skills

- fine motor coordination
- cause and effect

Telephone Time

It never fails; as soon as the telephone rings your climber gets into something he shouldn't. Assemble a box of special toys that are only available when you are on the telephone. Store the "telephone box" someplace where only Mom or Dad can get it down. The novelty keeps the appeal for when you are on the telephone.

Suggested toys include puzzles, shape sorters, nesting cups, small blocks, and magnetic shapes. (Be careful that these pieces are not too small to be swallowed.) These are all toys that have parts that can become lost. It is better to store these toys where they can be controlled by you, rather than left in a toy box or on a shelf.

Materials: storage box, special toys

Developing Skills

- grasp and release
- problem solving
- tactile discrimination

Cupboard Play Space

Climbers like to be where you are. Sometimes, it is hard to keep a climber interested in the same space you need to spend time, especially the kitchen. Try this: designate one of the kitchen cupboards as his. Store interesting objects there like plastic containers with tops, a few pans with lids, wooden spoons, or other toys. Mount a small chalkboard on the inside of the cupboard door. Let him use chalk or use a little bowl of water with a paintbrush to paint the board.

Materials: varies

Developing Skills

- cause and effect
- fine motor skills
- eye-hand coordination

Finger Plays

The following set of activities primarily involves the hands. They are done while sitting. Try them when your baby is in his high chair, car seat, while waiting in the grocery line, or at the doctor's office. Baby will not try to copy you at first. Baby will learn by watching you. Do not underestimate observation as a learning tool. After you have introduced a finger play by demonstrating it, hold baby in your lap, place your hands over his and move his hands through the motions. He will probably enjoy this stage for quite a while. After several repetitions, encourage your baby to do the finger plays along with you. It is best to face your baby at this stage to help him see what to do. Eventually your baby will be able to imitate your actions, however imprecisely. By the end of the climber stage he may know a few simple finger plays well enough to do them by himself while you say the words. Finger plays remain a fun challenge that children enjoy through the preschool years.

One Potato, Two

One Potato, Two

One potato, two potato, three potato, four
Five potato, six potato, seven potato, more
Eight potato, nine potato, ten potato, then
Let's start over and do it again.

(Pound your right fist on your left fist, then left over right, right over left, continuously to the rhythm of the poem.)

Variation: Repeat the poem very slowly; match the pounding to the new rhythm. Repeat the poem quickly. Say, "Let's try it even faster." Continue until neither one of you can keep up!

Developing Skills

- fine motor coordination
- tempo and rhythm
- exposure to counting

Ram Sam Sam

Developing Skills

- fine motor coordination
- multi-cultural music experience
- tempo and rhythm

Materials: none

This traditional Moroccan chant adds a few more actions, building on ones that your baby already knows.

Ram Sam Sam

A ram sam sam, a ram sam sam
(Pound fists right over left, left over right.)

Guli guli guli,
(Roll hands around each other.)

Ram sam sam
(Pound fists.)

(Repeat the verse.)

A rafi a rafi,
(Lift both hands overhead and wriggle fingers.)

Guli guli guli,
(Roll hands around each other.)

Ram sam sam.
(Pound fists.)

(Repeat the second verse.)

Whoops Johnny

Developing Skills

- tactile stimulation
- fine motor coordination
- tempo

Whoops Johnny

Johnny, Johnny, Johnny, Johnny

(Tap baby's right index finger on the tips of the four fingers on his left hand starting with his pinky.)

Whoops Johnny,

(Slide the right index finger down the side of the left index finger, continuing to the tip of the thumb.)

Whoops Johnny,

(Slide the right index finger back down the side of the thumb, continuing to the tip of the index finger.)

Johnny, Johnny, Johnny.

(Tap baby's right index finger on the tips of the three remaining fingers on his left hand ending with his pinky. Repeat with the other hand.)

Variations: Substitute baby's name for "Johnny." Use your finger on baby's hand.

Five Plump Peas

Five Plump Peas

Five plump peas in a pea pod pressed.
(Hold out one closed fist.)

One grew...Two grew...
(Thumb emerges... index finger emerges.)

So did all the rest!
(Extend all five fingers.)

They grew, and they grew, and they grew and never stopped.
(Open both arms wider and wider.)

They grew so fat that the pea pod popped!
(Spread arms as wide as possible and then clap loudly.)

Developing Skills

- fine motor coordination
- imitation

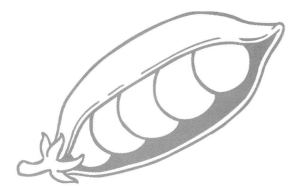

Materials: none

This finger play adds a few more movements. It is surprisingly difficult for baby to isolate and move his fingers independently. He may need to play along by simply opening and closing his hands.

Open, Shut Them

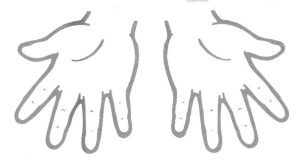

This is a great finger play for filling time while sitting and waiting at a restaurant, a bus stop, or a doctor's office. The best part is hiding your fingers at the end. Baby will want to do it again and again!

Developing Skills

- fine motor coordination
- vocabulary enrichment
- following directions

Open, shut them. Open, shut them.
(Start with two closed fists extended in front of you. Open your fist to fully extend all fingers; close fists. Repeat.)

Give a little clap, clap, clap.
(Clap three times.)

Open, shut them. Open, shut them.
(Open and close fists.)

Put them in your lap, lap, lap.
(Pat your lap three times.)

**Creep them, crawl them,
creep them, crawl them,**
(Walk fingers up your chest.)

right up to your chin, chin, chin.
(Stop hands under chin.)

Open up your little mouth—
(Open mouth.)

but do not let them in!
(Quickly hide fingers behind your back.)

Baby's First Play Dough

Play dough provides valuable sensory and fine motor experiences for your child. However, at this age most climbers will want to put it in their mouths. The following recipe is non-toxic. You may want to add a strong flavor extract like coffee or almond to discourage baby's tasting. Use play dough as a "we play together" experience. With your supervision, baby can explore and enjoy safely.

Play Dough

- 2 1/2 cups white flour
- 1/2 cup salt
- 2 1/2 tsp. alum
- 2 cups boiling water
- 2 Tbsp. oil
- food coloring and flavor extracts as desired

Combine the dry ingredients in a bowl. Stir the liquids together before pouring them into the bowl. Stir until the mixture is very stiff; then knead it with your hands until the dough is uniform and smooth. Play dough will last for weeks if it is stored in an airtight container or resealable bag.

Play Dough Ideas

- Always use rich language to complement your activities. Include words like *squishy, soft, squeeze, pull, poke,* and *stretch.*
- Embed small, safe toys in the dough. Let baby pull them out.
- Encase a small, safe toy inside a ball of dough. Let baby dig it out.
- Let baby stick golf tees or pegs in the dough.
- Roll out a thin layer of dough. Drive toy cars across to make tracks.
- Make impressions of kitchen utensils: potato masher, slotted spoon, plastic fork, etc.

Materials: play dough, tools or toys

Developing Skills

- fine motor coordination
- sensory exploration
- vocabulary enrichment

Build a Sentence

Now that baby can say a few words, help him build on what he knows. When your baby says a single word, repeat it within the context of a full sentence he would have said if he could. Baby says, "milk," you say, "Micah wants milk." Baby says, "Up," you say, "Pick me up."

Expand a Sentence

Add more information to baby's word, repeating it in a few sentences. Baby says "dog," you say, "See that dog! The dog is running. The dog is fast."

Developing Skills

- expressive language
- receptive language

Little Robin Red Breast

The next few activities (pages 205–207) are "whole body" finger plays. Following your movements requires focused attention. It is hard for a climber to "watch and do" simultaneously. He may watch several times before imitating the movements.

Developing Skills

- gross motor coordination
- imitation
- vocabulary enrichment

Little Robin Red Breast

Little robin red breast stood upon the rail.

(Stand with your hands tucked under your armpits. Flap your arms like wings.)

Needle, naddle went his head,

(Bob your head from side-to-side.)

Wiggle, waggle went his tail.

(Shake your "tail" from side-to-side.)

Materials: none

Donkey Old and Gray

Donkey, Donkey, Old and Gray

Developing Skills

- gross motor coordination
- imitation
- vocabulary enrichment

Remember, repetition is the key to learning at this age. Don't get discouraged if your climber doesn't join in right away. He is learning by observation.

Donkey, donkey, old and gray.
(Stand facing your child.)

Open your mouth,
(Open your mouth.)

and gently bray.
(Say, "Hee Haw.")

Lift your ears,
(Touch both ears with fingertips.)

and blow your horn,
(Say, "Hee Haw.")

to wake the world this sleepy morn.
(Raise your arms above your head, stretch, and yawn.)

Teddy Bear

Teddy Bear, Teddy Bear

Teddy bear, teddy bear, turn around.
(Start facing your child, then turn around.)

Teddy bear, teddy bear, touch the ground.
(Touch the floor.)

Teddy bear, teddy bear, stand up tall.
(Stand up.)

Teddy bear, teddy bear, crouch so small.
(Crouch down with arms wrapped around knees.)

Developing Skills

- gross motor coordination
- following directions
- vocabulary enrichment

Teddy bear, teddy bear, reach up high.
(Stretch both hands over head.)

Teddy bear, teddy bear, wave good-bye.
(Wave bye-bye.)

Teddy bear, teddy bear, show your shoe.
(Touch you shoe.)

Teddy bear, teddy bear, I love you!
(Rub noses or hug.)

There are many commands to follow in this game. You may want to play it with your baby in your arms first. He will see, feel, and learn all the motions as you take him through it. Soon he will be ready to follow along and copy you.

Bottle Bowling

Focus your climber's endless desire to move with this game. Place four or five bowling pins (plastic bottles) on spots on the floor marked by snippets of masking tape. Show your climber how to roll a ball to knock down the pins. He may want to set them up again, placing each pin on a tape spot. Encourage him to repeat the activity. This can be played indoors or outside.

Variation: Make pins from empty facial tissue boxes. Stack them in a pyramid shape for baby to knock down.

Materials: 4–5 plastic beverage bottles or tissue boxes, ball, masking tape

Developing Skills

- gross motor development
- cause and effect
- fine motor development

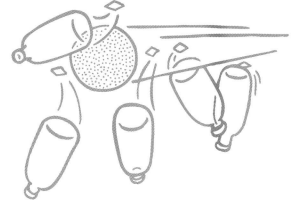

Shake It!

Make a shaker from the homemade instrument suggestions on page 210, to accompany this lively song. It may be easier for your baby to shake one in each hand simultaneously. Isolating arm movements separately requires bilateral coordination.

Variation: You can shake your hands at the wrists and clap on "Hey."

Materials: rhythm band instrument

Developing Skills

- bilateral coordination
- exposure to music
- following directions

Shake It!

I was going to Kentucky,
I was going to the fair,

to see a señorita, with flowers in her hair.

Oh, shake it baby, shake it,
shake it if you can.
(Shake your instrument in front of you.)

Shake it like a milkshake
and pour it in the pan.
(Tip your shaker to pantomime pouring.)

Oh, shake it to the bottom.
Shake it to the top.
(Shake low to the ground. Shake above your head.)

Shake it round and round and round,
until it's time to stop, Hey!
(Shake in a circle in front of you. Abruptly stop.)

Rhythm Band Instruments

- Drill or poke a hole through three juice can lids. Attach them together loosely with a chenille stick (pipe cleaner).
- String together several jingle bells on a chenille stick (pipe cleaner).
- Make a tambourine by putting dried beans inside two paper plates. Tape or staple around the edges of the plates to seal in the beans.
- Make different sounding shakers by putting dry rice, sand, beans, or noodles inside plastic screw top soda bottles.

Materials: juice can lids, jingle bells, pipe cleaners, dried beans, paper plates, stapler or tape, any size plastic soda bottles **Caution:** Rhythm band instruments should be stored out of reach when not in use.

Treasure Collage

Climbers love to walk, especially if they are not hurried, and can stop and explore at will. Bring a small pail with you to the park. As you explore, pick up little treasures along the way—feathers, small pebbles, leaves, twigs, etc. Name each object for your baby as you find it. After you get home, show your baby how to place each object on a piece of shelf paper. Name them again. Now is a great time to also talk about what the word "sticky" means. The finished artwork will look lovely hung in a window.

Materials: outdoor objects, clear shelf paper, small pail

Developing Skills

- gross motor coordination
- fine motor coordination
- vocabulary enrichment

Active Play

Climbers

Falling Leaves

Developing Skills

- sensory experiences
- gross motor play

Falling Leaves

(Sing to the tune of "Row, Row, Row Your Boat.")

Leaves, leaves, leaves in the air
(Lift hands above head.)

Swirling red and brown.
(Spin around.)

Leaves, leaves from the trees,
(Drop hands to sides.)

Falling to the ground.
(Drop body to the ground.)

Materials: leaves

Fall leaves provide rich experiences for your climber: crunch them, throw them, make piles to jump in, smell them.

One for the Money

Developing Skills
- gross motor coordination
- anticipation and waiting

One for the Money

One for the money,

Two for the show,

Three to get ready,

And four to go!

Use this chant to prompt your climber during outdoor play.

Examples:

- Stand on a curb together. Hold his hand. On the word "Go," jump off the curb.
- Lay a stick on the ground to jump over.
- With baby in a baby swing, pull back. Release the swing on "Go."

Active Play

Climbers

Little Caterpillar

Little Caterpillar

**Caterpillar, caterpillar,
go inside.**

(Roll child up.)

**Come out now
as a butterfly!**

(Unroll and flap your wings.)

Developing Skills

- gross motor coordination
- following directions

Teach your climber how to log roll. Lay on a carpeted surface with your arms at your sides. Roll over a few times. Have your climber lay down. Roll him over gently with your hands. After he can roll independently, play this game. Lay him on a towel. Make sure his head sticks out past the edge of the towel. Say the chant as you roll him up inside and unroll him. Say the first line of the chant as you roll him up again. Can he unroll himself?

Materials: a clean dry bath towel

Balloons in a Bag

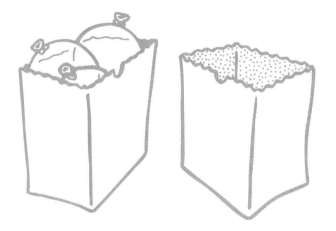

Climbers love to carry things as they walk. This activity is a gross motor version of a transfer activity. Put the balloons in one of the bags. Place the other bag about ten feet away. Show your climber how to pick a balloon out of the bag, carry it over and drop it into the second bag. Encourage your climber to transfer the balloons back to the first bag. Narrate his activity: "Now you're carrying a balloon. You dropped it in a bag. Can you get another one?" He can explore in and out and back and forth as long as he desires.

Caution: Balloons that are not inflated, and popped balloon pieces, are serious choking hazards. Always supervise this activity and remove materials when finished.

Materials: 4–5 balloons, two paper shopping bags

Developing Skills

- receptive language
- gross motor coordination
- spatial relationships

Obstacle Course

Climbers love to climb! Create an indoor obstacle course with pillows, couch cushions, a blanket over a table, chairs, etc. Play "Follow the Leader." Prompt your climber with language rich in prepositions. "Let's climb *over* the pillows." Accentuate and repeat the prepositions to reinforce them. "We went *over* the pillows!" Continue playing. "Let's go *around* the ottoman. Here we go *between* the chairs. Now, we are *under* the table."

Materials: "obstacles"

Developing Skills

- gross motor coordination
- vocabulary enrichment
- spatial awareness

Variation: Let your child freely explore the area while you narrate his movements, accentuating the prepositions *in, over, through, under, behind,* etc.

Hide and Seek

Object permanence really hits home when your baby causes the disappearance. Start by telling your baby "Let's play peek-a-boo. I will look for you." Walk out of the room and then call to him. "Where are you? Where is my little one? I'm coming to find you." Return to locate your baby. The more surprise in your reaction the better. It is a big joke now and he will giggle at your surprise every time.

Soon your baby will hide in all the familiar places he learned from you. A climber often hides in plain sight with his hands over his eyes. It is his egocentrism that allows him to believe that if he can't see you then you must not be able to see him. This is FUN!!!

Materials: none

Developing Skills

- gross motor play
- object permanence
- vocabulary enrichment
- self-awareness

Bubble Wrap Stampede

Secure a piece of bubble wrap to a hard floor by taping the wrap down along the edges. Show your climber what happens when you step on it. Let your climber stomp on it with bare feet. Use rich language. Include words like *pop, crinkle, stomp, plastic,* and *bubble.*

Caution: Always remove the bubble wrap immediately when finished. Never let your baby handle or chew on any type of plastic wrap to avoid a suffocation or choking hazard.

Materials: bubble wrap, wide masking tape

Developing Skills

- gross motor coordination
- tactile stimulation
- auditory stimulation

Boxes, Boxes, Boxes

Big boxes make great playthings. Appliance boxes make play houses. Cut a door and some windows out. Maybe your climber would enjoy decorating the sides by scribbling with markers. Smaller boxes (apple crate size) make great vehicles. Add a paper plate steering wheel and baby will climb in and drive. You can also turn boxes into a kitchen set. Draw some burners and knobs for a stove; cut a door for a cupboard or refrigerator. All of these ideas require more imagination than store-bought versions. They are better at promoting representational, symbolic thinking.

Developing Skills

- gross motor coordination
- conceptual thinking
- pretend play

Materials: boxes

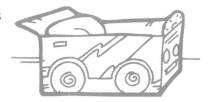

Tape Ball

Developing Skills

- fine motor coordination
- gross motor coordination
- tactile stimulation

Materials: masking tape or double stick tape.

Wrap masking tape around on itself with the sticky side out to make a ball about two inches in diameter. Make sure the ball is too big to fit in baby's mouth. Let your baby explore this unusual tactile sensation of stickiness. Stick the ball on different surfaces for baby to pull off. Stick it high on the refrigerator door so he has to reach up, on the underside of a table so he has to climb under it, on the floor, on his shirt or anywhere!

Variations: Cover a tennis ball or a Ping-Pong ball with double-sided tape.

Flip Over

Climbers love to experience their bodies in motion. This is a safe way to introduce the elements of a backward somersault. Sit on a chair with baby in your lap, facing you. Extend and stiffen your legs with your feet on the floor, like a slide. Lay baby down on your outstretched legs. Baby should be face up with his head toward your feet. Gently flip him over; hold him around his torso with your hands positioned as shown. Twist your wrists as he flips his legs over to land on the floor. Once he gets the hang of this, it will be a favorite.

Developing Skills

- gross motor coordination
- anticipation

Variations: Use the rhyme "Five in the Bed" from page 91 or "One for the Money" from page 213 to give baby verbal cues to associate with the action.

Materials: none

Step Stool Climber

The climber is in constant pursuit of climbing higher. This can be dangerous. Substitute an appropriate place to practice climbing, rather than saying "No" all the time. This will help get through this important stage of development pleasantly.

Purchase a folding step stool. Choose a model with a handle that comes over the top step. When your climber enters the room and begins to climb where he shouldn't be climbing, offer the step stool instead. You will need to stay close by at all times. Place the stool near a window where he can watch outside while climbing up and down. This can be a delightful way to spend time. **Variation:** Let baby watch you work in the sink washing vegetables or dishes.

Materials: step stool

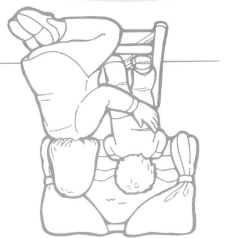

Developing Skills

- gross motor coordination
- spatial awareness
- bilateral coordination

Sliding Safety Rule

Climbers love to slide. It is difficult for a climber to discriminate which side of the slide to climb up. They like to go up both directions. You will need to teach your climber the safety rule. The only way he will learn is for you to be consistent. Every time he tries to climb up the slide end, gently pick him up and place him on the ladder. You can also stand in his way at the bottom of the slide and verbally encourage him to go up the ladder. Some say it is necessary to do something sixty consecutive times before it finally becomes a habit. Some say two thousand times! Skill development takes lots of practice, guidance, and encouragement. Positively reinforce him "Yippee! You went down the slide." or "You remembered to go up the ladder."

Here is a chant to help.

Up the ladder, down the slide.

Up the ladder, down the slide.

Developing Skills

- gross motor coordination
- following directions
- understanding limits

Two Naps to One

Sometime during this stage of development your climber will go from needing two naps to just one nap. Set up a good night's rest by regulating the time of the day and the duration of the nap. If the afternoon nap is over before 3:00 P.M. it will be easier to get baby to bed at night. Naps lasting past 3:00 P.M. interfere with bedtime.

For a while it seems the preferred naptime is over the lunch hour. Your little one may fall asleep at eleven and wake up at one. That is a good two-hour nap. Just keep stretching the start time by fifteen minutes. Serve lunch at 10:45, after a week serve lunch at 11:00 then 11:15. It may take a month or so but your climber will settle into one long afternoon nap rather than two short ones.

Developing Skills

- trust
- reinforcing routines

Bedtime Basket

Using ritual is the best way to help your climber make transitions. Create a bedtime basket. It will become a place to keep his "lovey" or pacifier during the day. By now, your climber has more than a few favorite books. He may insist on reading every one before bed. Keep from engaging in a power struggle by limiting the size of the basket to one that only two books can fit in it for bedtime story time. This way of organizing your bedtime ritual will help you take it on the road. Something will remain familiar. It will make traveling with your climber a little easier.

Materials: basket, books, special toys

Developing Skills

- language stimulation
- social development
- understanding limits

Glossary of Developmental Skills

Auditory discrimination: The ability to tell sounds apart. Recognizing one voice from another, rhyming words, or distinguishing letter sounds requires auditory discrimination.

Auditory stimulation: Presenting any sounds to baby, and focusing her attention on them. Listening to music or noisemaking toys stimulates auditory development.

Auditory tracking: The ability to identify the source of a sound or follow a sound as it moves through the environment.

Bilateral coordination: The ability to coordinate the movements of both sides of the body to produce smooth movements like crawling or walking.

Body awareness: Learning body parts and recognizing them as part of you.

Bonding: Developing an emotional connection to someone through consistent love and care. This is the foundation for trust and critical for healthy development in all areas.

Cause and effect: Exploring the consequences of a given action. Understanding that the same action results in the same effect.

Cross-lateral movement: The ability to move your hand or foot over to the opposite side, crossing the midline of the body.

Glossary of Developmental Skills (cont.)

Eye-hand/eye-foot coordination: Coordinating the movement of your hand or foot with the information you receive visually, like distance and speed of a moving object. Catching and throwing require this type of coordination.

Emotional awareness: The ability to recognize feelings and distinguish one feeling from another.

Expressive language: The extent to which you can communicate your thoughts to others. This can be non-verbal (gestures, body language, crying) or include the use of words.

Fine motor coordination: Controlling the muscles of the wrist, hand, and fingers in a purposeful way. Required skill to pick up or manipulate small objects, turn knobs, push buttons, or feed self.

Grasp and release: A fine motor skill that develops from a reflex grip at birth and evolves to a Palmer grasp, then a Pincer grasp.

Gross motor coordination: Controlling the large muscles of the body in purposeful movements like rolling over, sitting, crawling, walking, running, kicking, throwing, catching, and jumping.

Language stimulation: Any activity that presents language to baby: talking, reading aloud, responding to babbling.

Glossary of Developmental Skills (cont.)

Object permanence: A cognitive skill that allows baby to understand that things still exist even when they aren't in sight.

Palmer grasp: The ability to pick up an object between the fingers and the palm with or without the use of the thumb.

Pincer grasp: The ability to pick up an object between the thumb and index finger.

Pre-literacy skills: Any activity that promotes understanding of language and its written form: looking at books, listening to stories, learning rhymes, and rhythms of speech.

Pre-verbal communication: Any form of communication baby can use before she can talk well: crying, gestures, pointing, sign language.

Range of motion: Moving muscles through the full extent of their range stretching them to increase flexibility.

Receptive language: The extent to which you can understand words spoken to you, as well as voice intonation and inflection.

Reinforcing routines: Repeating a sequence of events or tasks to promote recall, memory, sequencing, patterning, and anticipation and security.

Glossary of Developmental Skills (cont.)

Self-awareness: Understanding that you are a separate being.

Self-calming routines: Providing for the development of skills that baby can use later to sooth herself.

Sensory stimulation: Providing a variety of things for baby to touch (tactile), taste (gustatory), smell (olfactory), hear (auditory) or see (visual).

Sensory discrimination: The ability to tell sensory input apart (color, texture, sound).

Sensory motor play: Experiences that integrate movement and tactile experiences: playing in sand, swimming, playing with play dough.

Spatial awareness: Knowing where your body is in space without visual cues. For example, we can walk down stairs without looking at each one and avoid obstacles while walking.

Spatial relationships: Understanding concepts of *under, over, through, next to, behind, below, near far, up, down*, etc.

Glossary of Developmental Skills (cont.)

Tactile stimulation: Providing varied sensations for baby to feel with her skin, fingers, lips or tongue.

Trust: The foundation for healthy emotional development that is built through consistent, predictable responses to baby's needs for food, warmth, security and closeness.

Vestibular system: The system in your body that helps you maintain balance and a sense of right-side-up. Part of this system is sensed in the inner ear.

Visual discrimination: The ability to tell things apart by how they look (e.g., color and patterns).

Visual memory: The ability to form a mental image of something seen.

Visual tracking: The ability to follow the movement of an object with your eyes.

Visual stimulation: Providing a variety of things for baby to look at: colors, shapes, shiny things.

Vocabulary enrichment: Building the number of known words through repetition and exposure.

Understanding limits: Knowing that some choices are not available.

Developmental Milestones

In general, babies develop their skills in a predictable sequence. The actual month in which a particular skill is attained varies. There is a wide normal range. For example, some babies walk as early as nine months, others as late as eighteen months, with the average falling around thirteen months. Anywhere in this broad range is considered normal. Every area of development has ranges of normal. It is best to pay attention to the "sequence" rather than fret about specific monthly goals. However, an individual's progress may not follow the typical order or include every step. Developmental rates are prescribed by an inner biological timetable. Your baby will grow and develop at her optimum rate with support and encouragement from you. You cannot speed up her development any more than you could control the rate at which she gets her teeth. The best you can do is provide exposure to new skills and opportunities to practice. The rest is up to your baby. Trust her. Relax and celebrate the person she is.

Developmental Milestones (cont.)

Gross Motor Sequence

Lifts and turns head, holds head up, lifts chest off the floor when on her tummy, rolls over from tummy to back before back to tummy (usually), sits with support, sits without support, pulls to a stand, scoots on tummy, crawls, walks around furniture (cruises), stands alone without support, stoops to pick up objects, walks unaided, climbs stairs.

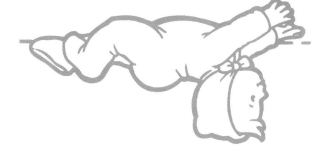

Fine Motor Sequence

Reflex grip at birth, opens and closes hands, reaches for toys, picks up objects with a Palmer grasp, mouths toys, passes objects from one hand to the other, bangs objects together, picks up and releases object with a Pincer grasp.

Developmental Milestones (cont.)

Language Sequence

Coos, babbles, squeals and laughs, uses different cries for different needs, responds to own name, mimics sounds, understands a few words receptively, tries to imitate words, can say a few single words.

Social-Emotional Sequence

Eyes follow parent, smiles in response to parent, initiates smile, communicates needs by crying, settles into patterns of eating and sleeping, reaches for familiar people, likes social games, anticipates feeding by opening mouth. Shy with unfamiliar people at first, plays peek-a-boo, cries when parent leaves, gives hugs and kisses, waves hello or goodbye, experiences full range of emotions.

Reaching Milestones

One way to help baby reach the next milestone is to practice the previous ones. Try some of the activities listed under the following skills.

Gross Motor Skills

Lifts Head: Follow That Sound 24, Look Up Here 27

Lifts Chest: Tummy Time 89, Getting Ready to Crawl 95

Rolls Over: Five in the Bed 91, Rolling Over 92

Sits: Sit-ups 42, Reach for the Sky 68, Creepers section Lap Games 74–82

Pulls to a Stand: Hop Little Bunny 88, Stand Up Song 93

Scoots: Foot Pushers 47, Hop Little Bunny 88, Scoot, Scoot 96

Crawls: Getting Ready to Crawl 95, Crawling Challenge 129, Surprise Pictures 130

Cruises: Look Who's Pointing 141, First Walker 166, Just Cruisin' 170

Stands: Stand Up Song 93, Stand and Deliver 167

Stoops: Jack in the Box 163, Stand and Deliver 167, Boxes, Boxes, Boxes 219

Walks: Push and Pull 171, Monster Rocking 176, Knee Walking 177

Fine Motor Skills

Intentional grasp: Crinkle Sock 25, Tummy Time 89

Reaches for toys: Tickle Me 18, Reach for the Sky 68, Potato Chip Can 90

Passes objects from one hand to the other: Not Enough Hands 69, Tug of War 131

Grasp and release: Baby's Own Spoon 66, Toy Overboard 109, Ping-Pong Bath 110, Where Is the Lid? 113, Kitchen Fun 145, Spindle Toy 175, Telephone Time 194

Pincer grasp: Snack Time Fun 108, Tear it Up 118, Mealtime Madness 146, Dipping 147, Use Your Finger 159

Language Skills

Coos and Babbles: Cooing and Babbling 31, Playback 32

Understands a Few Words: Nursery Rhymes, Poems, and Songs for Active Play 34, Peek-a-Boo 83, Bath Time 111, Throw the Ball 128, Kitchen Fun 145, Washing Dolly 149, Find Teddy's Nose 154, One Noun, One Verb 184, Preposition Play 189, see Songs 205–207

Says a Few Words: Picture Perfect 121, Good Night 137, Look Who's Pointing? 141, Build a Sentence 204

Index of Activities by Skill

Cognitive Activities

Cross-Lateral/Bilateral Coordination

Index of Activities by Skill (cont.)

Eye-Hand or Eye-Foot Coordination

Fine Motor Activities

Gross Motor Activities

See the Active Play sections

Index of Activities by Skill (cont.)

Index of Activities by Skill (cont.)

Index of Activities by Skill (cont.)

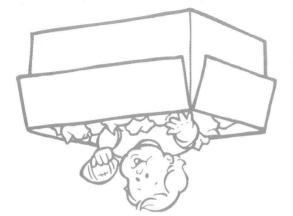